Other Novels
The Fifth Doll
Magic Bitter, Magic Sweet
Followed by Frost
Veins of Gold
The Will and the Wilds
The Hanging City
Still the Sun

Writing as C. N. Holmberg
You're My IT
Two-Damage My Heart

Dedicated to the dreamers,
to anyone who's ever pretended to have wings,
or thrown fireballs, or danced on water,
or imagined, for just a moment, they could do something
extraordinary.

CHARLIE N. HOLMBERG'S
BOOK OF MAGIC

OF

MAGIC

THE ULTIMATE FANTASY AUTHOR'S GUIDE TO MAGIC SYSTEMS

WALL STREET JOURNAL BESTSELLING AUTHOR

CHARLIE N. HOLMBERG

Charlie N. Holmberg's Book of Magic
COPYRIGHT © 2024 Charlie N. Holmberg

Interior Illustrations by Andy Loiseau

Published by Oliver Heber Books
0 9 8 7 6 5 4 3 2 1

TABLE OF CONTENTS

OTHER BOOKS BY CHARLIE N. HOLMBERG

FORWARD BY
BRIAN MCCLELLAN

———～～———

"She'd always had a thing for fantasy,
for magic and make-believe."

–*Soul of Smoke* by Caitlyn McFarland

Writing is a strange, sometimes fraught medium. It
is highly praised and undervalued; a combina-
tion of science and art that can determine our
relationships with friends, coworkers, spouses, bosses, and
even the general public. People agonize for hours over
just a text or a work email. They spent thousands of dol-
lars on writing seminars and masterclasses—money well
spent, for the way we use language is constantly evolving
on both a personal and societal level. Even the professionals—especially the professionals—are always on the
lookout for ways to refresh and expand their communication toolset.

If you're reading this book you aspire to something truly great—to create whole new stories that may be hundreds of thousands of words long and include fantastical elements that you whipped up in your head and now wish to inject into the heads of others.

Storytellers, by their very nature, are scientists, madmen, and alchemists even before the characters they label as such make their way to the page.

I first met Charlie at Brandon Sanderson's house. We were there for a short interview and photo session for BYU magazine; an angle on showcasing his successful students. The interview was fun. I seem to remember Charlie and I were barely mentioned in the actual article. It was kind of a formal occasion, so we really didn't get to chat. But we did keep in touch.

It's been really neat getting to know another career author who literally comes out of the same school of writing. It's been especially neat because Charlie writes romantic fantasy. The world of romance writing has always seemed somewhat distant and mystical to me. I write rambling action books and am an appalling romantic in real life. A friend who actually understands that world? Yes, please! She's always happy to give me advice when I'm struggling with the romance angle of my books. And Charlie is fun to hang out with. She leaves me rolling on the ground laughing with the wild things she says. The only predictable thing about her is that she'll get cranky if game night goes much past 9 p.m.

She's an incredibly talented author and a hard worker. I'm serious. It's a work ethic I would kill for. She gets out multiple books a year. Real, well-written books with deep worlds and complex characters and, of course, lots of kissing. Do you know how hard that is to produce that much quality content? I thought I was doing well getting out a book every sixteen months or so with Powder Mage. On top of all that, she teaches writing classes and goes to conferences and gives advice to other authors.

She's dispensing a lot of that advice in this book. Magic systems, however simple or intricate, are the backbone of fantastical stories. If you're writing anything with supernatural elements, a whole bunch of questions are going to come up: how much does magic affect my story? When should I use magic to solve problems? Do I want it to be mysterious, or thoroughly codified? Charlie helps you understand what questions are going to come up and how to answer them.

Good information is like taking a shortcut to being a better writer. It's amazing when you're learning to write. It's even better after you've found success. Most pros I know keep a shelf of writing advice books for personal reference. I certainly do, and this one is going to be on it.

—Brian McClellan, author of the Powder Mage and Glass Immortals series.

1
INTRODUCTION

———~~———

"And yet, is magic not merely the act of
creating something from nothing?"

–*To Poison a King* by S.G. Prince

First, I'm really impressed you're reading the opening
of this book. I usually skip them.

Second, welcome to my dense and express book
on writing magic systems. I adore magic. The majority
of the novels I write start with my developing magic,
so it's been a crucial (and fun) element of writing for
me since the beginning. I truly believe having a well-
thought-out and intriguing magic system elevates any
fantasy novel, and sometimes the magic alone can be a
pitch for the book itself. (I've 100% pitched my Numina
series as "magical fidget-spinners meets Pokemon.")

That said, you do not need to have a complex magic
system to have a wonderful, even bestselling, novel.
There are many stellar books on the shelves with simple

magic that read and sell beautifully (*Touch of Power* by Maria V. Snyder, *Soulless* by Gail Carriger, and *Burning Glass* by Kathryn Purdie, for starters).

While I definitely do want you to read this book, I will also note that you don't need to have *any* magic whatsoever to have a great fantasy novel. A book falls into the fantasy genre just by being *other*, whether that's other-world, other-creature, or whatever otherness your mind conjures. Books like Tricia Levenseller's *Warrior of the Wild* and Danielle L. Jensen's *The Bridge Kingdom* are great examples of this.

Magic also doesn't have to take over your story—sometimes just a pinch of it is needed for a premise to work, such as creating a curse in *Daughter of the Forest* by Juliet Marillier. (The sorceress who cast it is never seen again—her presence is there to instigate the curse that provides the catalyst for the story. It's literally one of my favorite novels.)

Magic is like Everything Bagel seasoning—it can bring out the best of anything. Setting, plot, and character can all be intrinsically wrapped up in a sharp magic system that hammers home twists and climaxes. Magic can let you explore that *otherness* to its fullest and let your mind—and the minds of your readers—explore worlds and tales they'd never have a chance to experience otherwise. And, frankly, magic is *fun*, so why not?

I personally hate wading through pages of fluff to get to the gold in craft books (I was an English major. I basically have a degree in wading through fluff), so I've tried to keep this book succinct. All meat. And, if you've already been through the magic roundabout a dozen times, I have worksheets and appendices in this book meant to spur brainstorming and generate ideas for future magic systems. Hopefully these can be a tool for you now and into the future.

Anyway. I said no fluff. So, let's get on with it, shall we?

2
TWO SCHOOLS OF MAGIC: LIMITED VS. UNLIMITED

—⟪⟫—

"This is magic skillfully woven."

—Genevieve Gornichec, *The Witch's Heart*

When looking at magic, we first need to determine what overall type of magic we're using. Magic systems, in general, can be divided into two categories: limited (hard) magic and unlimited (soft) magic.

Limited Magic is magic that operates within strict parameters. It utilizes a strict set of rules, has a small and focused breadth, and possesses specific costs and consequences (more on that in Chapter 4). Limited magic can be explained in its entirety; the reader knows exactly how the magic works. It's almost scientific in its nature.

Unlimited Magic, in contrast, possesses broader parameters and a much looser set of rules. It's wide in scope, can vary in costs and consequences, and sometimes is not fully explained (but shouldn't be infinite[1]). Unlimited magic is often an essential part of the world, like air or water.

SCHOOLS OF MAGIC	
Limited	**Unlimited**
Strict set of rules	Loose set of rules
Narrow scope	Broad scope
Specific costs/consequences	Varies in costs and consequences

This is not to say you can't have a limited magic system that's an essential part of the world, or that you can't have an unlimited magic system with specific costs and consequences. Because I've also just lied to you. Magic systems are far more than two simple schools of magic. They're on a spectrum. But to understand the spectrum of magic, you need to first understand the endpoints of that spectrum.

LIMITED MAGIC   UNLIMITED MAGIC

Pull out any magic system from any book, and it will fall somewhere on this spectrum. Authors like Brandon Sanderson tend to veer very close to the left, while

---

1   The only infinite magic system I've seen is that in Bruce Almighty, where the point of the premise was for an ordinary man to have literal god-like powers.

authors like Dianna Wynne Jones tend to veer closer to the right. Some magic falls right in the middle, such as J.K. Rowling's Harry Potter series. The magic in this series has some very specific requirements, such as wizards needing specific lineages, wands, and incantations pronounced *precisely* for a spell to take. But J.K. Rowling could also write a new Harry Potter book tomorrow and slap in whatever spells she wants to make her story work—the amount and types of spells in this series is nearly endless.

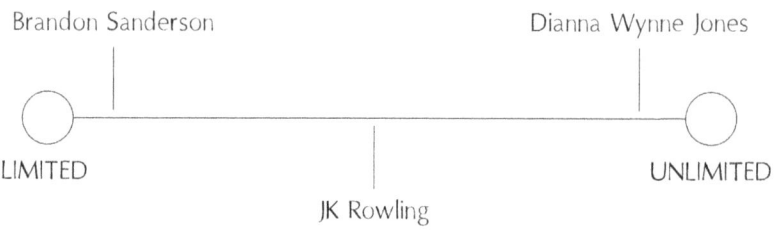

Further right on the spectrum, between Harry Potter and the Castle series, we might find something like *Twilight* by Stephenie Meyer. Generally speaking, vampire and other species-specific novels tend to lean more limited. They have specific creatures (vampires) made in specific ways (biting) with specific powers (super strength) and specific costs (goodbye sunlight). But Meyer put a spin on her version of vampires that shifts her closer to an unlimited magic system. While she does have specific rules concerning her vampires, such as how they're created and how they notoriously sparkle in sunlight, she added the creation of magical gifts upon turning—gifts tied to natural abilities the vampire possessed while human. For example, the series's lead man, Edward Cullen, was quick footed as a mortal, so he's especially fast as a vampire. Another character, Alice, had psychic abilities as a human, and they're greatly magnified after she turns.

This amplification of natural ability into the super-natural is done in such a way that there's a near endless scope of possible vampire abilities in the Twilight-series world. Someone sensitive to smell could turn and have the nose of a bloodhound. A contortionist could turn and essentially become Elastigirl (of Pixar's *Incredibles* fame). This element of possibility skews *Twilight* far more unlimited than many of its vampiric counterparts.

Opposite that is my own Paper Magician series. Looking solely at the magic introduced in the first book, *The Paper Magician,* there are many strict rules that pull it closer to the limited side of the spectrum. People can only do magic with a very specific set of man-made materials, such as paper, glass, and plastic. Once a magician is bonded to their specific material, there's no return. Spells are one word and must be recited aloud. Folds, as is done in paper magic, must be precisely creased and perfectly aligned. However, this magic system is not truly limited, because like Rowling, I could write another book in the series and introduce entirely new spells never-before mentioned in the rest of the series. The scope of those spells is somewhat limited, as the materials a magician has to work with can only logically[2] do so much. But there is definite wiggle room there.

(If each faction in The Paper Magician series had, say, only ten spells each, set in stone, I would have a truly limited magic system on my hands.)

---

2 I mean, as "logical" as magic and fantasy gets...

Using these examples (plus a couple more), our spectrum would look something like this:

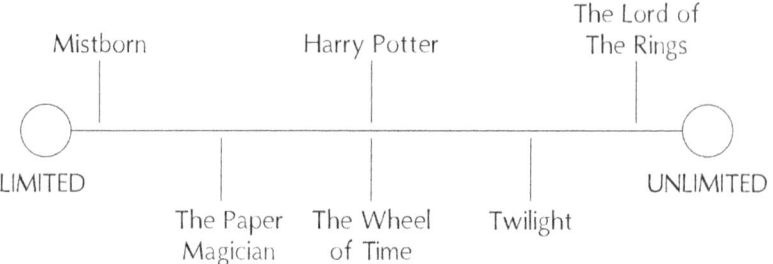

Now that we understand the spectrum, we can graduate to yet another metaphor: a sound board.

Yes, I've lied to you again—ish. Really, we're just moving our view of magic from something two-dimensional to something three-dimensional. So now, I want you to picture magic as a sound board—those complicated things you see music producers using in movies on the opposite side of the glass from where our star is singing.

Essentially, any element of magic—structure, cost, fuel, whimsy—is a dial, knob, or switch on our proverbial sound board. You can dial them up and down as you see fit. You can add levers to your liking. You can even turn some of them off, if you'd prefer. More of this in Chapter 4. I've included an example here.

SOUNDBOARD OF MAGIC

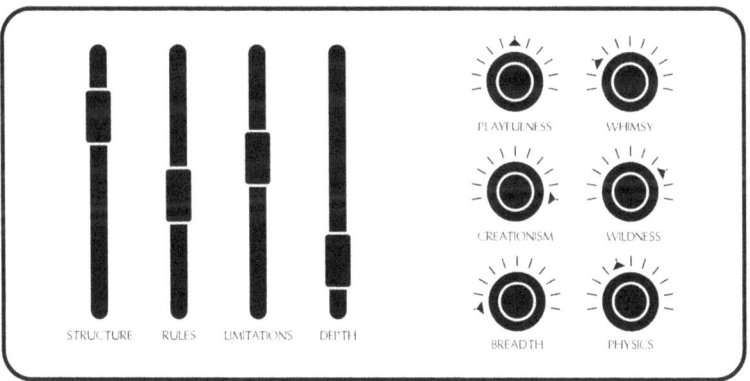

JUST A SPRINKLE

Not all books with magic need full-fledged magic systems. Sometimes a premise needs just enough magic to kick off a story. I took a note from Juliet Marillier and established the existence of magic just enough to curse my protagonist in my novel Followed by Frost. There's enough worldbuilding to know that wizards exist, but outside of the curse, they aren't pertinent to the story. While I could dive deeper into the magic system of this book, it's just not necessary for the plot.

Notes:

_____

_____

_____

_____

_____

_____

_____

_____

_____

_____

_____

_____

_____

_____

_____

_____

_____

_____

_____

_____

_____

3
SANDERSON'S LAWS OF MAGIC

—◦◦◦—

"Magic can only do so much."

—The Hundred Thousand Kingdoms by N.K. Jemisin

We can't talk about magic systems without talking about Brandon Sanderson.[3]

I mean, we definitely *could*. There's a lot of amazing magic systems out there begging to be admired and studied. But Sanderson is a champion of limited magic systems—if having a tight, rule-bound magic system gets your passion flowing, I highly recommend reading his books. However, what I moreso want to discuss is Sanderson's three laws of magic, which apply to

---

3 Sanderson, Brandon. "What Are Sanderson's Laws of Magic?" Brandonsanderson.com. Dragonsteel Publishing. 2018. https://faq.brandonsanderson. com/knowledge-base/what-are-sandersons-laws-of-magic/.

all magic systems—limited, unlimited, and everything in between. These laws of magic can guide any fantasy writer, beginner or expert, in writing a magic system that proficiently adds to storytelling. These rules are as follows:

1. An author's ability to solve conflict with magic is directly proportional to how well the reader understands said magic.
2. Limitations are greater than powers.
3. Expand what you already have before you add something new.

So, let's discuss.

Law One: An author's ability to solve conflict with magic is directly proportional to how well the reader understands said magic.

Let's say we're writing a novel that utilizes a plant-based magic system. In this magic system, Green Mages have the ability to make plants grow at will. The ability to point-and-shoot, so to speak. Green Mage sees a blade of grass, points her magic at it, and the green blade of grass grows far faster than it naturally would. A sprout becomes a full blade in a matter of seconds. However, a Green Mage can only grow a plant as large as the plant naturally grows. So, if we're magicking a blade of Kentucky Bluegrass, the maximum length it can grow is twenty-four inches.

Following me? Great.

Now, let's say we have this great idea for the climax (the big THING at the end) of the book, where our Green Mage is going to tie the bad guy up with an enormous rope of Kentucky Bluegrass. We need it to happen quickly, so the Green Mage can't just take a timeout and start weaving together a grass rope in the corner while the villain patiently waits for his defeat. We also can't utilize a longer-growing plant, like an elephant creeper, because for REASONS this climax needs to happen in the Green Mage's backyard in rural Montana, where no elephant creepers grow. So, it would be pretty cool if our Green Mage could just super-size a blade or two of Kentucky Bluegrass and wrap the bad guy up in that, winning the day. However, according to Sanderson's first law of magic, our protagonist can't just point her fingers and make the grass grow, *even if we offer a magical explanation as it's happening.*

Why? Because that flexibility with the magic has not been introduced to the reader beforehand. The foreshadowing has not been established, and now our climax is incredibly disappointing. Hello, one-star review.

To introduce this climactic flexibility, you'll need to introduce the possibility of expanding this spell earlier in the book. However, that doesn't mean you must include a scene where the Green Mage successfully grows a blade of Kentucky Bluegrass a mile long—no, that would take out the *oomph* and surprise of our climax. However, we can leave clues, a la foreshadowing, throughout the book so that, when the big magic happens, the reader understands how and why it came to be.

Okay, Charlie. What clues are we talking about?

Well:

- Maybe there's a prophecy of a great Green Mage who can expand the walls of plant magic, and there are subtle things within that prophecy that align with our protagonist.

- Maybe there are also magic users in this story who utilize water magic, and our Green Mage studies under them and learns basic concepts that, if she could only master them, would allow her to grow plants even larger than their natural limitations allow.

  ¤ Maybe one of these water wizards is her long-lost father, so she already has the magic within her, or

  ¤ She befriends a water wizard and learns to combine their abilities.

- Perhaps in the story, the Green Mage makes a deal with a demon to increase her powers, and it *seems* that deal fell through, or she got the short end of the stick. Until the climax, where some aspect of the demon's riddle suddenly makes sense, and the Green Mage is finally able to grasp the added magic just in time to save herself.

I could go on. We could brainstorm pages and pages of ideas so that we can plant seeds (pun absolutely intended) throughout the book for a big, magical payoff in the climax, without spoiling the payoff early.

Law Two: Limitations are greater than powers.

In a nutshell, this means that what the magic *can't* do is often more interesting than what the magic *can* do. So yes, it's neat that our Green Mage can go around and make plants grow really fast. Our first chapters could be filled with her going to impoverished villages and saving their harvests, then working as a contractor for a paper mill, replenishing trees in demolished forests. She could discover her friend is sad and sprout up a bouquet of flowers for her. She could take a rest on the side of the road and instantly grow herself some shade.

But after a while, this is going to get old. By chapter five, six, or ten, readers are going to start thinking, "Oh yeah, cool, she grew her dinner again. I wonder what I'm having for dinner. I should figure that out," and close the book.

Adding limitations, as discussed in Chapter 2, makes a magic system more dynamic. So, what can we do to make this magic system a little more exciting?

- Perhaps our green magic only works in sunlight. Photosynthesis and all that.

- Perhaps the acceleration of the magic comes from the Green Mage's body, so it saps her energy.

Now, say our Green Mage finds herself at the end of a long journey, battle, or other exhausting occasion, and she's desperate for food. But it's February, the sun sets at 6:03 p.m., and she can't grow her dinner. Or there's a trickle of sunlight left, but she's so exhausted that by the time she's done sprouting ingredients for soup, she passes out. On the side of the road. In bandit country (because why not).

- What if to grow one plant, you had to kill another?

So Green Mage grows herself some vegetable soup, not realizing that down the road, she just murdered the fledging garden of a starving widow.

- What if to accelerate the life of one living thing, you had to quelch the life of another?

Maybe, in order to use her magic, the Green Mage uses her own physical growth as a battery, leaving her perpetually young. Not *fun* young, like I'm-one-thousand-years-old-but-I'm-a-hot-twenty-something-forever. Nope—in reality, our Green Mage can't mature beyond the age of ten. She's been alive for forty-one years, but still looks like a child. That guy she's in love with back home? Not interested—it's creepy. Those children she's dreamed of having? She's not developed enough to carry them. So now she's choosing between saving the farms of peasants and living the life of a physical adult.

That sucks. And it's *awesome*. That's a story I would read. Because limitations in magic create conflict, and conflict makes books interesting. You can see here how the inclusion of magic could enhance our story—especially the internal struggles of our protagonist.

Law Three: Expand what you already have before you add something new.

Sanderson himself has created a perfect example of this in his Mistborn series. The original trilogy has three flavors of metal-based magic—allomancy, or people who eat metal to use magic; feruchemy, or people who wear metal to use magic; and hemalurgy, or people who pierce themselves with metal to use magic.

Let's look at (and vastly simplify) the first two: we have a person with allomancy (allomancer) who can eat steel and subsequently use a pushing force on anything made of metal. The laws of physics apply; if our allo-mancer, who weighs 180 lbs., pushes against a metal folding chair, the metal folding chair will move forward, because it weighs less than he does. If he pushes against a Toyota Prius, the allomancer will move backward, because the Prius weighs more than he does.

Now let's look at our person with feruchemy (feruchemist). She has the ability to store her weight in metal. She also weighs 180 lbs. But she can store some of that weight in her bracelet and walk around as though she weighs ninety. The longer she stores that extra ninety lbs., the more weight she accumulates in her bracelet. Then, later, when the driver of that Prius falls asleep at the wheel and sends his car hurtling toward a stroller, our feruchemist can stand in the way, tap into all her stored bracelet-weight, and suddenly have a mass of several tons. She blocks the car and saves the baby.

Are you with me? Yes? Good. No? Uh … pretend, then.

So. This is the very concise version of the magic in the original Mistborn trilogy. But then Sanderson decided to write more books in the Mistborn world, only three-hundred years in the future.

Now, we want these books to be exciting! We want to do something new. Sanderson could have tacked on a fourth metal-based magic, maybe something discovered during those three-hundred passing years. (Uh … metallic tattoos or inhalers or something.) But instead, he made his allomancer and his feruchemist have BABIES.

So now we have a crossbred magic user. Let's name him Shannon. Shannon weighs 180 lbs. and is standing in a room with a metal folding chair. If Shannon eats steel and pushes magic into that chair, the chair is going to move forward. But now, Shannon also has the ability to store his weight in his iron bracelet. So, Shannon shoves 175 lbs. in there and now, when he pushes on the folding chair, Shannon goes backwards. Shannon has a lot more options with his pushing magic than his great-great-great grandfather ever did, because he can control his mass.

I.e. Sanderson expanded what he already had before he added something new.

Let's apply this to our Green Mage. Green Mage has struggled with her limitations and uncovered a secret way to grow plants beyond their natural size at the end of book one. Now we're onto book two, and we want to focus on magic once more for a twist. How do we find something new within the magic system we've already created without tacking on something novel (again, pun intended)?

- Perhaps our Green Mage learns to focus her magic downward, growing out the *roots* of the plant as opposed to the stalk/leaves/etc. She can use this magic to, oh, keep a mine from collapsing or find underground water in a drought.

- Perhaps our Green Mage realizes that if she's touching the skin of a family member, she can quelch *their* growth instead of her own when she uses magic. Now her body can finally age, but at what toll to her family?

- Perhaps the Green Mage discovers maple trees and, using her newfound abilities to overgrow plants, she creates an enormous maple syrup farm and becomes a world leader by selling tree-sugar like cocaine to visiting aliens (yes, this is a reference to *Live Free or Die* by John Ringo. And yes, I realize this isn't really an expansion within the magic system, but I entertained myself with it anyway).

There are dozens and dozens of possibilities, depending on how long and hard you want to brainstorm. (For more on this, see the section on originality in Chapter 4.) You are not required to delve deep enough into magic systems to utilize this law in your books; fantasy novels are fantasy because they contain some sort of *other*, whether that be in setting (i.e. enchanted forest), character (i.e. fairy), or the existence of magic.[4] However, if you're going to make your magic system a large part of your plot, then this law needs to be taken into consideration. As does our fourth law:

Charlie N. Holmberg's First Law of Magic: The more ingrained a magic system is to your plot, the deeper that magic system needs to be.

In other words, if you want a light magic system in your book, something to give the story flavor or make your protagonist or villain especially cool, then great! Have at it. But if you want to do as our Green Mage does and use magic to solve multiple and/or complex conflicts, as well as have large swathes of plot reliant on the magic, then you need to dig deep into the magic so a) it all makes sense in the end, and b) you don't dig yourself into a plot hole (ever been in a writing group where

---

4 Yes, I realize magic is part of setting, but it sounds prettier and clearer this way.

someone asks, "Why didn't they just do X spell to get out of this?" That's what I'm talking about).

What deepens a magic system? Well, everything we've talked about up to this point, for starters, plus everything we're talking about for the next two chapters of this book. You can also include the origin and history of the magic as well, especially if you're writing a series. The more fodder you give yourself, the more books you can write without having to stress and sweat over how to stretch your magic to the very last novel.

If you don't want spoilers for my Numina trilogy, skip to Chapter 4. (Or better yet, go read the Numina trilogy and then come back to finish this book.[5])

The whole reason I wrote the Numina trilogy was actually professional pressure—I loved writing stand-alones, but my editor wanted another series from me. So, I pulled out every idea I had that was interesting to me at that moment, and I smooshed them together to make a story. And, of course, I started with the magic system.

For a magic system to be plot relevant, with all the fun twists and revelations I wanted to have, and carry over three books, it had to be a deep magic system. In book one, I introduce readers to two different magics: a talisman magic (see Chapter 6) that granted its holder one minute of immortality every twenty-four hours, and a summoning magic, where a summoner could use the bodies of slaves to bring monsters into the world (surprise, he's the bad guy). By the end of the book, both of my protagonists lose their respective magic and there is much sadness.

In book two, I play in my magic sandbox and leave

---

5 Self-promooooooootiooooonnnnnn~~~

some more breadcrumbs for readers. My slave (a vessel) learns how to become a summoner. We discover god is actually one of these monsters. And we learn that the talisman can be paired with a summoner to bring extreme beings onto the mortal plane.

In book three, I get to dig into the history of everything—where the magic came from, and why it's morphed the way it has. You learn that the two abilities—the immortality and the summoning—are actually directly related. I get to send one of my protagonists to the plane of monsters and reveal that the monsters used to be human. I also get to show the macabre way a talisman is made and use it to solve conflict in the final battle.

If your magic system ends up being *big* when you create it, you very likely have a series on your hands. If not, you can write a standalone novel, or simply don't base so much of the plot on your magic system. The choice is yours.

4

BUILDING YOUR MAGIC SYSTEM

―――

"Nothing is free, nothing is safe.
Magic always comes at a cost."

―*One Dark Window* by Rachel Gillig

Originality

Before we get into the bones of building a magic system, I want to take a page or two to discuss originality.

Originality really is what separates a lot of books and a lot of authors. In fantasy, it's tempting to default to an "easy" magic system so we can focus on storytelling. This isn't necessarily a bad thing—if I want to start my story *in medias res*[6], with a man being assaulted by a vam-

―――

6 Meaning "in the middle" of the action.

pire in an alleyway, all I have to do is say "vampire" and the antagonistic force is set. I don't have to waste time grounding the reader, because vampires are so common, I can start the story with no learning curve. And if I'm trying to hook readers on the action, then this is absolutely a tool I'm going to use.

Books can employ simple or preset magic systems when the goal is flavor, highlighting power, or invoking a fantastical setting. Easy magic has a shallow learning curve, and therefore can attract more readers, especially those unused to the conventions of the fantasy genre. But for those who want magic to be a large part of the story—tied in deeply with characters and plot—take a moment to differentiate yourself from the books that may sit beside yours on the shelf (or above and below you on the Amazon scroll). Take your time with it—don't rush development. Great magic systems, like great stories, need time to marinate in your brain before they come to life on paper.

A few tips to spark originality:

Take note of what's currently saturating the market and avoid it. If you bank off writing to market, then jumping on the bandwagon of what's hot now can pay off in the short term. However, if you want something to stand out in one of the many slush piles of traditional publishing, or you want to guarantee your book will still be interesting ten years from now, consider taking the untrodden path.

Take a "done" magic and make it different. If your heart is set on elemental magic or powered-up tattoos, that's okay! Just put a unique twist on it. This is what Stephenie Meyer did with *Twilight*. She took vampires (done, done, and done) and made them her own. This is also why you can have two books with seemingly similar magic systems and have completely different stories. Case in point, both Brent Weeks' Lightbringer trilogy and Brandon Sanderson's *Warbreaker* use color-based magic. But the magic is explored in such fundamentally different manners that the casual reader would never dream of comparing them.

In regard to my Paper Magician series, I wasn't the first person to think of magical origami (though at the time, driving in my car between Idaho and Utah, I thought maybe I was). Paper magic is also in the 1999 manga series *Read or Die*, for instance. But my expanding paper magic into the realm of manmade materials made it unique. If you're trying to turn heads, you don't need an entirely unique, never-seen-before magic system (or hey, let the book's premise be the unique element and go ahead and write about fairies or fire or whatever makes your id[7] happy). You can have something familiar with a unique twist or quirk.

Make a list. This process can be done with any aspect of brainstorming, not just magic. Make a list of whatever it is you need to figure out, such as what kind of creature will innately possess magic in your story (more on this in Chapter 6). And just start vomiting out ideas. The further down the list you get, the harder your brain is working, and the more original your ideas will be. (Note that going *too* far down the list might leave you with something too bizarre to realistically work with.)

---

7 A la Freud: id, ego, super-ego. The id is your carnal
   desire, your impulses, your pleasure center.

For example, here's a list of potential magical creatures for my theoretical story:

1. Unicorns
2. Vampires
3. Pegasi
4. Flying frogs
5. Flying fish
6. Giant bats
7. Giant butterflies
8. Wolves with butterfly wings
9. Forest-eating caterpillars
10. Three-headed snakes

Based on that list (which I literally did write off the top of my head and have not changed from the rough draft of this book for the sake of reality), I really like the idea of forest-eating caterpillars. And they can transform into giant butterflies, so that's a two-for-one.

Remember, more often than not, simpler is better. It's really easy for us to go overboard with our worldbuilding and open a giant can of worms that will devour and suffocate our readers, so it's important to keep it simple. Take a moment and think of the best magic systems you've read in your favorite books. More likely than not, you could explain them to someone quickly and concisely. Getting too complex with magic steepens the learning curve and frustrates readers.

Rule of thumb? If you, the author, have to continually look at your notes to remember how your magic works, your reader isn't going to stick around to learn it.

Cost and Consequence

So, limitations are more interesting than powers. But what kind of limitations are we talking about?

Limitations are things that make performing, owning, creating, or other verb-ing the magic *hard*. They're the reason why Luke can't just force-lightning the Death Star into oblivion and Gandalf can't just teleport the ring into the heart of Mount Doom. Limitations create sources of conflict for the characters and the story they're telling. They enhance the story. A majority of these limitations fall into the realm of *cost*.

What is cost? <u>Cost is the fuel needed, or the toll taken, when a person uses magic.</u> Cost should be inherent in both schools of magic, regardless of where on the spectrum your novel sits. Cost is something that should never be dialed to zero on our metaphorical sound boards, unless magic is so exceedingly rare or naturally limited in your world that it doesn't matter. More often than not, however, your story isn't an exception. Magic should always have cost. How much, and how dire, is up to you. Cost is generally associated with a magic's fuel and/or toll.

A "fuel" for a magic system is something required for the magic to work: a vial of blood, the rays of the sun, or a twinkie from the cupboard. In Brian McClellan's *The Shadow of Lightning*, the fuel needed is a specific kind of sand (cindersand) that's melted down into magical "godglass." Magic users, called "glassdancers," can't control just any glass; it has to be, *specifically*, godglass. However, cindersand is a limited resource, and it's nearly run out. No cindersand, no godglass, no magic. An instant limitation is placed on the magic system simply by making its fuel difficult to acquire.

If you're stuck on ideas for costs or fuels for your magic system, Appendix A at the back of this book has a list to help jumpstart some ideas.

A "toll" for a magic system is a consequence of using the magic, often given to the magic user herself, but not always. Rachel Gillig, in her The Shepherd King series, has a two-fold magic system; both halves come with notable cost. The first type of magic comes from catching a fever from the deadly mists that surround Blunder, the town in which our protagonist lives. If a man gets the fever and his veins turn black, the fever will leave a magical ability with him. The first cost of this magic is socially constructed, in that magic is viewed very negatively in this world, and the evil Destriers and Physicians will take you away. The second is that use of this kind of magic causes degeneration in the infected, often in the form of mental or physical decay.

The second magic system is performed through a series of Providence Cards. There are twelve types of cards in total, with different types being rarer than others. Anyone can use these cards, and each type of card contains a specific ability, such as granting its user beauty, combat skills, or the power to control others. However, there is definitive cost attached to these cards, and the consequences are as unique as the cards themselves. A person overusing the card of beauty becomes ugly inside. Overusing combat prowess makes the user weak, and overusing the control of others causes intense physical pain.

Limitation is created in a magic system when the consequence hinders the ability to use magic in one way or another.

When creating toll in a magic system, ask yourself who is paying the toll.

In Rachel Gillig's The Shepherd King series, the person using a Providence Card receives the toll first-hand.

In contrast, Richard Matheson's short story, "Button, Button," introduces a simple button that, if pushed, will grant the pusher a large sum of money. The toll is that someone, somewhere, in the world will die. In this case, the person using the "magic" is not experiencing the cost themselves (or they do, indirectly, if you decide you want to pick up the story and read it for yourself).

A more extensive example of delegating the toll of magic can be found in David Farland's Runelords series. In these books, the magic user (a *Runelord*) doesn't pay the physical costs of magic himself, but rather employs (if doing so ethically) donors to bear the cost in his stead. For example, if a Runelord wants to double his strength, that additional strength must come from a donor. The strength is transferred from donor to Runelord, leaving the donor pathetically weak. The Runelord now has the charge of housing and caring for this donor, especially considering that, if the donor dies, the Runelord will lose the gifted strength. In this case, one could argue the direct toll to the Runelord is actually financial, as he must have the ability to nurture and protect his donors. There is also the added consequence of ignoring physics (i.e. having amplified strength, but not amplified constitution, means you can lift a car over your head, but you'll break your bones doing so).

Weakness

There is one more category limitations can fall into, and that is *weakness*. A weakness in a magic system is something that hinders or nullifies the magic. The most classic example of this is Superman's kryptonite. When this handy green crystal is around our overpowered superhero, his magic ceases to exist. Kryptonite is therefore this magic system's weakness.

In Jeff Wheeler's Muirwood series, magic stems from a source known as the "Medium." This Medium can be harnessed as a Christian might harness the holy spirit, or a Jedi, the Force. However, the power of the Medium will shy away from any whose thoughts are fearful or selfish. Therefore, fear and selfishness are weaknesses of the magic (or moreso, of the magic user).

If a magic user is charged by the sun, then clouds, a solar eclipse, and nightfall would be their weakness. If a mage can only move with her mind what she can physically move with her body, then physical lack of strength would be her weakness.

In Susanna Clark's *Piranesi*, using magic is so complex that it bars most people from being able to access it.

Another means of looking at weakness could be the danger involved when using magic. For example, in the popular table-top game *Dungeons and Dragons*, a wizard can cast a spell as a ritual, but it takes ten minutes to complete, leaving that wizard susceptible to attack from enemies for ten rounds of combat.

We can also, for the sake of plot, look at social weaknesses magic might create. In "Lady of Pain," a short story by Steven DuBois, magic users have the ability to heal. However, a healed person must still experience all the suffering associated with their illness or injury, so when he is healed, he feels all of it at once. It's excruciating, and because of that, healers are socially hated, despite the good they do.

This is essentially a way to say that weaknesses (along with fuels and tolls) can come in a variety of shapes and sizes. A magic system doesn't *require* a weakness—that's something that can be dialed down on the sound board. But it's certainly a means of creating limitations for a story. However, while limitations in magic are critical, there's more to magic than what it can and can't do, and from here, we'll work on the functional building of a magic system.

Acquisition

Acquisition is a crucial part of any magic system and is often one of the elements taken for granted in the brainstorming phase. You can get pretty wild with how your characters acquire magic in your story, but here's a summary of macro-level means of acquisition I've seen around:

1. *It's in your blood.* Magic is inherited; it's part of your genealogy. At least one of your parents (or grandparents, or uncle) was a magic user, therefore you are also a magic user. This type of magical acquisition is very popular because it's easy and logical. The Harry Potter series by J.K. Rowling utilizes genealogical magic.

2. *It's in your species.* If you were born an elf, a fairy, a goblin, etc, you get the magic specifically associated with being that species. The Lord

of the Rings series by J.R.R. Tolkien utilizes species-specific magic. (See also the section on exclusive magic in Chapter 6.)

3. *It's infecting you.* If you were bitten by a werewolf, or you got the magic-based disease that's been festering in your neighbor's cabbages, you now have the magic associated with that disease. Most vampire and werewolf books fall into this category. Magic by possession also falls under this classification—perhaps you have demon powers because a demon is using your body as a vacation rental.

4. *It mutated you.* Maybe you were too close to that solar flare, or you drank the green ooze in the sewer. Either way, by accident or on purpose, that funky stuff has mutated you, and now you have superpowers. Many superhero origin stories (*The Fantastic Four, Teenage Mutant Ninja Turtles*) utilize mutation for magic.

5. *You chose it.* Sometimes we're very intentional with our magic. Sometimes any Joe Schmoe can go to the mighty wizarding library and study up to become a mage. Using magic is simply a choice you make, like choosing to become a doctor or a taxi-cab driver. The Discworld series by Terry Pratchett utilizes free choice for magic acquisition.

6. *You found an imbued object.* Whether a supernatural being gifted it to you, or you unearthed it in the bottom of a riverbed, you found a magical object, and so long as you have that magical object, you have magic. The TV show *Miraculous Ladybug* utilizes imbued objects. (See the

section on magical talismans in Chapter 6.)

7. *You have access to a magical power source.* Maybe it's a pillar of light, or a sentient volcano, or a sleeping god, but it gives off an aura of magic, and if you've been exposed to it, you now have powers. *The Foxglove King* by Hannah Whitten utilizes exposure to a magical power source in this way.

8. *You got it from a magical creature.* You own a unicorn, or you killed a dragon, or you milk a necromantic goat every morning. Regardless, magic comes from a creature that you own/visit/kill/etc, and that's how you get your magic. *Dune* by Frank Herbert utilizes magic from magical creatures.

   8a. I will add a subsection to this where magic can also be taken from other magic users. A mage may have acquired his magic via one of the other methods listed, but another character got *their* magic by stealing it from the mage. "Hemalurgy" from the Mistborn series by Brandon Sanderson utilizes this kind of magical theft.

9. *You experienced trauma.* And something about that trauma created or unlocked something within you. Something that relates to or becomes magical. *The Poisons We Drink* by Bethany Baptiste utilizes trauma for magic.

10. *A deity gave it to you.* Your magic was a holy gift by some greater being. You're a paladin, or a disciple, or just in the right place at the right time. *The Wings Upon Her Back* by Samantha Mills utilizes holy gifts for magic. (See the sec-

tion on divine magic in Chapter 6.)

11. *You found a spellbook.* An actual tome, or whatever form spells take in your world. You found it, you read it, and you studied it. Now you can use it to cast magic. Often, spellbooks are complex enough that they must be in the hands of the magic user when casting. In this sense, spellbooks are not imbued objects, because they are not, in and of themselves, magical, merely a medium for magic to be used (the same way a cookbook is a medium for recipes to be used). *Practical Magic* by Alice Hoffman utilizes spellbooks. (See the section on witches and wizardry in Chapter 6.)

12. *You just … have magic.* It's random. Some people have magic, and some people don't. It can't really be connected to bloodline or location or anything scientific, it just is. The Wheel of Time series by Robert Jordan utilizes random selection for magic.

Here's a quick reference table:

Method of Acquisition	Examples from Literature & TV
Inherited/ Genealogy	Harry Potter series by J.K. Rowling, the Mistborn series by Brandon Sanderson
Species-specific	The Lord of the Rings series by J.R.R. Tolkien, The Infernal Devices series by Cassandra Clare

Infection	Most vampire and werewolf novels (*Soulless* by Gail Carriger, the Scarlett Bernard series by Melissa Olsen, to name a few.)
Mutation/ Accident	*The Fantastic Four* by Stan Lee and Jack Kirby, *Teenage Mutant Ninja Turtles* by Kevin Eastman and Peter Laird.
Free Choice	The Discworld series by Terry Pratchett
Imbued Object	*Miraculous Ladybug* by Thomas Astruc
Power Source	*The Foxglove King* by Hannah Whitten, *Stolen Songbird* by Danielle Jensen
Magical Creature	*Dune* by Frank Herbert, *Eragon* by Christopher Paolini
Trauma	*The Poisons We Drink* by Bethany Baptiste, *The Hanging City* by Charlie N. Holmberg
Holy Gift	*The Wings Upon Her Back* by Samantha Mills, the Animorphs series by Katherine Applegate
Spellbook	*Practical Magic* by Alice Hoffman
Random	The Wheel of Time series by Robert Jordan

Mind you this is not an exhaustive list, and even within these categories, there's a lot of wiggle room and opportunity for innovation. But if you're going to have characters with magic in your story, you should probably know how they got that magic in the first place.

Potency

Potency—power level, spell output, mana capacity—is the strength with which a person or creature is able to cast magic. How powerful a magic user are they? This can be tied back into acquisition if desired; perhaps a person born into a long line of wizards will have stronger magic than a bastard child from some powerless peasant, merely because magic is in the blood, and the "purebred" has more of it. Or, perhaps, a mage has lived all his life close to the source of magic, so he is a stronger magician than someone who's lived far away. But means of acquisition is not the only determiner—*if you have one at all*—for what makes a magic user stronger versus weaker.

When discussing potency, we mean the latent potential to do magic. Think of it this way: You have two completely different women who both want to swim for the Olympics. They both started swimming lessons at the age of five and had identical resources throughout their lives. However, by the time they reach the age of sixteen, one of them is six feet tall with broad shoulders and long limbs—an ideal body type for swimming—while the other is five-feet tall and rather petite. The former athlete is far more likely to be competitive in swim, merely because her genetics allow her to be so. It isn't any fault of hers, or the other girl's. She's just naturally a stronger swimmer.

That is how potency works in magic. It's the reason why Nynaeve from The Wheel of Time series by Robert Jordan excelled so quickly through the ranks of the Aes Sedai compared to other women who had studied longer and harder than she. The potency of her magic was simply stronger than that of her colleagues.

Potency in magic is not something that *must* be addressed in a magic system; static ability levels in magic is absolutely acceptable and fine[8]. Normal, even. But if you want to have some characters be inherently stronger in their powers than others, by means beyond practice and experience, you'll want a reason for why that is so. And yes, that reason could simply be *they were born that way*. But it's an opportune sandbox to play in.

Workshop

When I teach magic systems with a live class, I like to have students do a little workshop with me. The easiest way to do this workshop is to grab a bag close to you, or open a drawer, or obtain some kind of container with general stuff in it. From that container*, pull out something random—lipgloss, a stapler, lint ... whatever you touch first (or whatever floats your boat. There's technically no cheating, here).

---

8   This is not to negate the possibility that Magic User A might be more creative or clever with their magic than Magic User B. They may come off as more powerful because they're working smarter, not harder, when in reality the potency of magic is equal between magic users.

With that random object, I want you to create a magic system. Try to make it as book-able as you can (I understand that some silliness may ensue; feel free to embrace the comedy genre). Really take a moment to dig into it. You might come up with an idea that really sparks your imagination. Or, at the very worst, you'll get some practice.

Write the following across a piece of paper: *Power, Acquisition, Fuel, Toll, Weakness, Potency*, or just scrawl right into the table on the next page (There are more copies of this table on the following pages). You can include a miscellaneous column for other notes. Remember, you don't *have* to include every category in your magic system, but for the sake of the workshop, try to flesh out as much as you can.

Magic System Builder						
POWER(S)	ACQUISITION	FUEL	TOLL	WEAKNESS	POTENCY	MISC.

*If you're in a place or situation where you can't casually rummage through a receptacle, here's a list of random stuff you can choose from instead. For even *more* random suggestions to get your brain juices flowing, see Appendix D.

Needles	Thread	Fans
Butter	Picture frame	Knife
Mirror	Florescent light	Wire
Bread	Magnet	Perfume
Braiding	Compass	Bead
Chain	Clay	Wood
Flowers	Stones	Fruit
Clouds	Locks	Gasoline
Ink	Sugar	Animal skins
Salt	Piano keys	Fingerprints
Insects	Vitamins	Cups
Thorns	Hair	Piano keys

Magic System Builder						
POWER(S)	ACQUISITION	FUEL	TOLL	WEAKNESS	POTENCY	MISC.

Magic System Builder						
POWER(S)	ACQUISITION	FUEL	TOLL	WEAKNESS	POTENCY	MISC.

Magic System Builder						
POWER(S)	ACQUISITION	FUEL	TOLL	WEAKNESS	POTENCY	MISC.

Magic System Builder						
POWER(S)	ACQUISITION	FUEL	TOLL	WEAKNESS	POTENCY	MISC.

Magic System Builder						
POWER(S)	ACQUISITION	FUEL	TOLL	WEAKNESS	POTENCY	MISC.

Notes:

_____

_____

_____

_____

_____

_____

_____

_____

_____

_____

_____

_____

_____

_____

_____

_____

_____

_____

_____

_____

5
THE INFLUENCE OF MAGIC ON WORLDBUILDING

"Magic could be reckless, unpredictable,
and dangerous in the wrong hands."

–*The Witch's Lens* by Luanne G. Smith

A key element of a successful magic system is how it's integrated into the setting of the novel. The more well-known the magic, the more common the magic, the more it's going to influence the world around it. Once you've pieced together your magic system, consider how it will affect technology, religion, government, culture, and the workings of the world itself.

Magic and Technology

We're so accustomed to so many forms of technology in our day-to-day lives, we often overlook just how integrated technology is in our society. Depending on the nature of magic, it may replace some or even all technology, or vice versa (in Disney's *Onward*, magic was completely replaced with technology as society advanced). Do your characters turn on a faucet to get water, or can they congeal it from the air around them? Do they cook on a stove, or summon the power of the sun to fry their eggs?

The rule of thumb is this: people do what comes easiest for them. So, if magic simplifies a task, they're going to choose magic. If available technology simplifies a task, they're going to choose technology.

The following is not an exhaustive list of the ways magic could affect or enhance technology in your story, but a means of considering the larger ramifications of their relationship.

Occupations. Does the existence of magic create, alter, or destroy jobs? In *The Merciful Crow* by Margaret Owen, funeral rites were done exclusively by the lowest tier of magic users.

Communication. Does the existence of magic affect how messages are sent? Does it influence language, privacy, or other linguistically relevant matters? In The Stormlight Archives series by Brandon Sanderson, special pens could be linked to one another to allow two people to communicate over long distances.

Medicine. Does the existence of magic affect life expectancy? How does it hinder or advance population growth? How does it affect disease and injury, and who has access to it? In Stephenie Meyer's *The Host*, medicine was incredibly advanced and accessible to all. Most illnesses and injuries were easily remedied.

Economics. Can magic be purchased, or magic users paid for their services? How valuable is magic to society? Who can afford it? In *Howl's Moving Castle* by Dianna Wynne Jones, anyone can approach their local wizard and buy a spell.

Transportation. Does magic affect how a person gets from point A to point B? Does it allow for teleportation, or can it fuel engines or enchant wheels? In Robert Jordan's The Wheel of Time series, male channelers created rifts through an alternate dimension to form passageways for Ogiers. These "Ways" shorten the distance between two Waygates, minimizing travel.

Warfare. Can magic in your world affect warfare in any way, shape, or form? Because if it can, it will. Even the existence of better medicine can get soldiers back onto the field faster. Can magic be weaponized? Can it be used defensively? Can it get messages to generals quicker, or spy on enemy forces? In Brian McClellan's Powder Mage series, powder mages can use magic to extend the distance of a fired bullet.

Note that technology and magic can co-exist. Even the bridle and the wheel are technology. But, if you find yourself leaning harder into technological innovations as opposed to spells and enchantments, you might have a science fiction novel on your hands. Remember,

Magic + Technology = Fantasy novel

Science + Technology = Science fiction novel[9]

---

9 Though let's be honest, a lot of science in science fiction novels is a little magicky. Like magic-in-a-bad-wig-and-sunglasses magicky. But within the pages of this book, let's call it science.

Magic and Religion/Ethics

Every society has some sort of religion or ethical standard set in place. Even a land full of atheists still punishes murder or frowns upon lying. Religion and other belief systems allow for deep worldbuilding, and common or well-known magic can very easily play into this. There is a *lot* to consider when it comes to world beliefs. The following is very much a "nutshell" take on it.

Deity. Is magic attributed to gods or other greater beings, literally or figuratively? (Note that God doesn't have to be real for people to believe It is the source of magic.)

Leaders. Is magic attributed to priests, shamans, or other religious figureheads? Perhaps *only* these societal leaders are allowed to use magic, or only they know the source of it.

Sects. Do differing religious sects prescribe to magic differently? There may be opposing lore for its creation, different rules governing its use, or different magic used between sects entirely.

Ethics. Is magic dependent on one's nature? Does society only let those in good standing wield magic, or could wielding magic be considered sinful? Are there moral consequences for using, or for being caught using, magic?

Government and Politics

Again, the more commonplace magic is, the more it's going to affect society. It will *absolutely* affect how a city/country/nation is run.

Government. What laws govern the use of magic? If people know magic exists, they will find ways to restrict it, for better or for worse. There may be committees dedicated to monitoring and ruling over magic. Ask yourself if magic users can hold office, if they need to be licensed or otherwise educated, or if they're legal at all. You'll also want to address the economics of magic. Can it be bought and sold? Can magic be used as a career, or is it subsidized by the government? Money matters.

I will reiterate: if magic can be used for war, it will be. If it can be used for money, it will be. If it can satiate the greed of a person with any iota of power, it will be[10].

A great example of government's involvement with magic is Freya Marske's *A Marvelous Light.* A branch of the government, called the "Magical Assembly," is devoted to the registration and tracking of magic users. It has sub-departments too, such as the "Office of Special Domestic Affairs and Complaints," which reports directly to the Prime Minister. All magic users must be registered. All magic must remain secret—kept out of the press and the minds of those who might witness it. The government even keeps a lock of hair from every registered magician to aid them in keeping track of the magical community.

People and Culture

Even if magic has religious or political backing, the way people as a whole view, treat, or accept magic might not align with it. The *government* of Xyxxyz might allow magic and want to include it in everything, but the *peo-*

---

10 If it can be used for sex, it probably will be too.

ple of Xyxxyz might be wary of it. Or vice versa—the people could be pro magic, but the local government or religion wants to squash it for good, well-motivated reasons (like the classic "they want to stay in power" situation).

Taboos and superstition. This is a big one to play with, socially. Are there superstitions within the magic that magic users themselves practice? Are there taboos among non-magic-users in relation to magic and how it's used? (Let us all remember the taboo of naming the wizard that shan't be named in that very popular wizarding school series.) There is also the cultural perception of magic that is "off-limits," such as black magic. A magic user may have the ability to raise the dead but won't because of social ethics.

Language. Many magic systems have their own language or linguistic flare. If magic users require higher education or separation from society as a whole, they will likely have a different manner of speaking than nonmagical people. (Language is further discussed in Chapter 6, under *component magic*.)

Ethnicity/Nationality. Is magic tied to a specific people or nation? A la *Avatar*, we had, very specifically, the Fire Nation, the Water tribes, etc. Magic may be exclusive to a specific people who discovered it, or whose land possesses the source of magic. Magic may also be exclusive to specific peoples, by race, lineage, sex, or other factors (See *exclusive magic* in Chapter 6).

Social mannerisms. People behave differently around others they may see as an authority, dangerous, or different (like in the Milgram Experiment, where participants made choices that went against their own conscience because the person directing them wore a white lab coat, and thus appeared to be in authority). Determining where magic users are situated in society will determine how others treat them—whether it's with worship, respect, ire, or disdain.

Physical World

The fun thing about the fantasy genre is that it has license to do whatever it wants, so long as it can be reasonably explained. With that in mind, note if your magic system breaks the laws of physics, and why it's able to do so, (details can be dependent on how limited or unlimited your magic system is; see Chapter 2). Honestly, if you want to say magic can make people float without any explanation, we'll believe it, because the explanation is *magic*. But, depending on the story and how integral magic is to solving plot problems, you may want to explain or "hang a lantern[11]" on anything that breaks scientific principles in a way that will hurt a reader's suspension of disbelief[12].

---

11 "Hanging a lantern" on something is essentially purposefully pointing out an inconsistency or faux pas in a story to let the readers know *I'm aware, it's on purpose*, or *just wait—it will make sense later.*
12 "Suspension of disbelief" is where we're willing to forgo logic and critical thinking in order to buy in to the tale being told to us. "Sure, I'll believe this prince can be turned into a frog for the sake of enjoying and understanding this fairytale."

MAGIC AND THE WORLD BASICS WORKSHEET

Part 1

Technology

Does my magic system affect technology?
☐ Yes   ☐ No

If Yes:

_____

_____

_____

_____

_____

Types of technology affected:

_____

_____

_____

_____

_____

If No: Are you sure?

_____

_____

_____

_____

_____

Occupation
_____

Does my magic system create or cancel jobs?
   ☐ Yes   ☐ No

If Yes:

_____

_____

_____

_____

_____

What jobs does it create?

_____

_____

_____

_____

_____

Which jobs become obsolete?

_____

_____

_____

_____

_____

How much of the workforce will be affected by this?

_____

_____

_____

_____

_____

If No: Are you sure?

_____

_____

_____

_____

_____

_____

Communication

Does my magic system create new means of communicating?
☐ Yes   ☐ No

If Yes:

_____

_____

_____

_____

Is in-world modern communication altered or obsolete?

_____

_____

_____

_____

Is new communication available?

_____

_____

_____

_____

_____

How many people have access to this communication?

_____

_____

_____

_____

_____

Is this used in warfare?

_____

_____

_____

_____

_____

If No: Are you sure?

_____

_____

_____

_____

_____

_____

Medicine

Does my magic system affect medicine, healing, or longevity?
☐ Yes   ☐ No

If Yes:

_____

_____

_____

_____

_____

How does it work?

_____

_____

_____

_____

Who has access to it?

_____

_____

_____

_____

_____

How does this affect warfare?

_____

_____

_____

_____

_____

How does this affect population growth?

_____

_____

_____

_____

_____

If No: Are you sure?

_____

_____

_____

_____

_____

_____

_____

Economics

Does my magic system affect the economics of my world?
  ☐ Yes   ☐ No

If Yes:

_____

_____

_____

_____

Can magic be purchased separately from a magic user (item), or is it a service the magic user must be present for?

_____

_____

_____

_____

Is magic expensive or inexpensive? What affects the cost or inflation of it?

_____

_____

_____

_____

Who has access to purchasing opportunities?

_____

_____

_____

_____

_____

If No: Are you sure?

_____

_____

_____

_____

Transportation

Does my magic system affect how people move from point A to point B?
   ☐ Yes   ☐ No

If Yes:

_____

_____

_____

_____

_____

Does this magic affect modern in-world methods of transportation?

_____

_____

_____

_____

Does this magic replace previous methods of transportation?

_____

_____

_____

_____

How quickly can someone get from point A to point B as compared to walking, riding, etc?

_____

_____

_____

_____

Who has access to this transportation?

_____

_____

_____

_____

How is this used in warfare?

_____

_____

_____

_____

_____

If No: Are you sure?

_____

_____

_____

_____

Warfare

_____

Can my magic system be used in warfare?
   ☐ Yes   ☐ No

If Yes:

_____

_____

_____

_____

_____

What ways does it affect wartime uses of the categories listed above?

_____

_____

_____

_____

How can it be used offensively?

_____

_____

_____

_____

How can it be used defensively?

_____

_____

_____

_____

Does the opposing side have access to this magic?

_____

_____

_____

_____

Does this magic affect the holding or retaining of critical information?

_____

_____

_____

_____

Who has access to this magic?

_____

_____

_____

_____

What happens on the battlefield if the magic is used incorrectly?

_____

_____

_____

_____

If No: Are you sure?

_____

_____

_____

_____

Part 2

Religion and Ethics

Does my magic system affect the personal or group beliefs of any peoples in my story?

☐ Yes   ☐ No

If Yes:

_____

_____

_____

_____

_____

Is magic attributed to God(s)?

_____

_____

_____

_____

Is God(s) real?

_____

_____

_____

_____

Does magic actually come from heaven, or only believed to come from heaven?

_____

_____

_____

_____

_____

Do magic users have any level of authority in the world's belief system(s)?

_____

_____

_____

_____

_____

Is magic lauded or detested? Worshipped or feared?

_____

_____

_____

_____

_____

_____

_____

_____

What religious or ethical beliefs are taught about magic?

_____

_____

_____

_____

_____

Are they correct?

_____

_____

_____

_____

_____

How is magic treated among separate religions or sects, if any?

_____

_____

_____

_____

_____

_____

_____

_____

_____

What is the punishment or reward, religiously, for using magic?

_____

_____

_____

_____

_____

_____

_____

_____

If No: Are you sure?

_____

_____

_____

_____

_____

_____

_____

_____

Part 3

Government and Politics

What laws have been made regarding magic in my world?
The answer is only YES, unless,
Is magic so rare and unknown that laws have yet to be made about it?

_____

_____

_____

What specific laws govern magic in relation to the categories listed previously?

_____

_____

_____

_____

_____

What additional, special laws affect magic and magic users?

_____

_____

_____

_____

Is magic represented in government? How?

_____

_____

_____

_____

Is government involved in the creation and education of magic users?

_____

_____

_____

How do neighboring countries' laws differ from those central to the story?

_____

_____

_____

_____

Can magic users hold office?

_____

_____

_____

_____

_____

_____

People and Culture

How is magic viewed and treated among everyday civilians?
Do the people align with the religious and political views
on magic?

_____

_____

_____

_____

_____

What taboos or superstitions to people believe or practice in regard to magic?

_____

_____

_____

_____

Are they based in fear, truth, or something else?

_____

_____

_____

_____

_____

Are there special terms, or special languages, related to magic and/or magic users?

_____

_____

_____

_____

_____

_____

_____

Is magic specific to a specific type or class of people?

_____

_____

_____

_____

_____

Why?

_____

_____

_____

_____

_____

How are these people viewed and treated by those not in their group?

_____

_____

_____

_____

_____

_____

_____

What social rules have been erected in regard to magic and magic users?

_____

_____

_____

_____

_____

_____

_____

Notes:

_____

_____

_____

_____

_____

_____

_____

_____

_____

_____

_____

_____

_____

_____

_____

_____

_____

_____

_____

_____

6
TYPES OF MAGIC

———～～～———

"I slept for only a few hours in the mornings,
dreaming of magic that stained my hands like blood."

–*Nocturne* by Alyssa Wees

There is no perfect formula for a magic system. No must-have beat sheet or necessary structure. However, many popular magic systems do seem to fall into certain categories, and many of those categories have a framework to them. In this chapter, we'll dive into some of these frameworks so we can gain a better comprehension of successful magic systems in the fantasy genre.

Tiered magic

Tiered magic is as it sounds: magic is acquired in tiers, like a ladder (or a cake, if you're hungry). The idea is that the magic user starts on tier one, a.k.a the lowest tier, and must earn their way to tiers two, three, etc.

Tiered magic is one that often favors study, practice, and longevity, depending on the nature of its power source. Typically speaking, the amount of magic a user has correlates to the amount of experience they've accumulated.

Tiered magic is very popular in table-top roleplaying games, such as *Dungeons and Dragons*. Your character literally starts at "level one" and has to acquire experience throughout the game to reach higher levels, which come with a greater quantity and quality of spells (assuming you're playing a magic user, which in this scenario, of course you are).

Tiered magic is also popular in magic-school stories, such as the Witchlings series by Claribel A. Ortega. A student's proficiency and skill in magic dictates how high of a magical tier they can reach, and again, these tiers are labeled by numbers (level one, level two, and so on).

Sectional magic

Sectional magic is a magic system that possesses specific, clear roles for variations on magic and magic user; the magic is broken down into sections. This is a relatively popular framework to use for magic and can be seen in books such as *Mistborn: The Final Empire* by Brandon Sanderson and *The Black Prism* by Brent Weeks. For our purposes, we're going to look at *The Bird and the Sword* by Amy Harmon.

Harmon utilized a simple but powerful sectional magic system in this novel where magic users are divided into four specific categories (sections): Spinners, Changers, Healers, and Tellers. *Spinners* were those who could spin anything into gold; *Changers* could shapeshift into animals; *Healers* could, of course, heal others of injury and sickness; and *Tellers* had the ability to see into the future. Even after centuries of dilution and intermixing (see Sanderson's Third Law of Magic in Chapter 3), magic users can still be classified into one of these four sections.

There is no rule for the number of sections a magic system can or can't have; in this example, Amy Harmon used four, whereas Margaret Owen used five in *The Merciful Crow,* Brent Weeks used seven in *The Black Prism*, and Brandon Sanderson used sixteen in the Mistborn series (allomancy only, please no Sanderfans come after me for that number). However, a good rule for sections, as with anything magic or fantasy, is this: if you, the author, have to use a reference sheet to remember the different skills and abilities you've incorporated into your story, your magic system is too complex. More often than not, the simpler a magic system is, the better it will be (and the flatter you'll make the learning curve for the reader[13]).

Many sectional magic systems come with "umbrellas." An *umbrella*, in this case, is a magic user who encompasses all sections established in a magic system. An "umbrella" magic user wields all magic available and, is therefore, more powerful than any other individual magic user. The popular animated show *Avatar* is a simple and excellent example of this concept. *Avatar* utilizes a standard elemental magic system that incorporates "benders" of water, fire, earth, and air. However, there is, at any given time, one *avatar*, or an umbrella character who can control all four elements.

Umbrella magic-users are very popular (but not

---

13 Yes, I have stated this earlier in the book. MAYBE IT IS IMPORTANT, EH?

necessary) in fantasy novels with sectional magic. Who doesn't want to see a super-powered character utilize every tool in a magic system's proverbial toolbelt? The weight of consequence for this magic (see Chapter 4), lack of control over it, etc., can be great sources of conflict. Amping up the available magic can enhance both the magic system itself and the story's other elements.

Some magic systems, such as chromaturgy from Brent Weeks's The Black Prism series, also utilize *partial umbrellas,* or magic-users who can control multiple sections of a magic system, but not all of them. This series uses a light-based magic system, naturally sectioning it into the various types of visible and invisible light. Different colors of light can be turned into different "luxins," which are essentially used as building materials. For example, magic-users (called *drafters)* can use red light to create a sticky, tar-like luxin, whereas green light creates a flexible, albeit rough, luxin. Some drafters are partial-umbrellas (called *polychromes*), who are able to control two, three, or even four colors of light individually. Above all these is the *Prism,* or the full-umbrella character that can control all seven colors (Weeks fans, don't get on me for that number either, I know it expands to eleven[14] later in the series, sheesh!).

---

14 Eleven might seem like an especially high number of sections for a magic system, but given that these sections are based on the colors of the rainbow, which most of us memorize at a very young age, chromaturgy has a relatively shallow learning curve. Weeks is also smart in that he doesn't expand into this higher number of sections until later in the series, thus giving us ample time to adjust to the magic system, thus flattening the learning curve.

Nonsectional Magic

Nonsectional magic is, somewhat obviously, the opposite of sectional magic, where all magic users have access to the full bounty that is magic. We can see an example of this in *Jade City* by Fonda Lee, where magic users (*Green Bones*), once they've graduated from rigorous magic training, have access to all the wonders magic has to offer them. While you could argue that magic with more than one ability or power is "sectioned" (in this example, the ability to deflect, super speed/strength/hearing, sensing auras of others, etc), the Green Bones themselves are not differentiated one from another. Any Green Bone typically has access to all the magic[15]. Therefore, they are nonsectional.

Exclusive Magic

Exclusive magic is rather straightforward: it is magic specific to a species or class. Example, if you are X species/class/gender/what-have-you, you will have Y abilities. Taking examples from the Court of Thorns and Roses series by Sarah J. Maas, if you are *daemati*, you will have mind powers. If you are a *seer*, you have future-sight. If you are a *shadowsinger*, you have shadow magic. Cut and dry, maybe she's born with it; maybe it's Maybelline™.

---

15 Some Green Bones are more proficient at specific aspects of the magic, yes, but they still have full access to the magical spectrum.

Crossbreeding and Dilution

Let's say the species in our fictional fairyland are fae and elves, each with their own brand of magic. What happens if these creatures intermix? This is where we have to ask ourselves questions and have painful flashbacks of ninth-grade biology Punnett Squares—diagrams used to determine probable genotypes in offspring. Is one magic dominant over another (i.e. a fae/elf mix always results in elf powers)? Will the magic nullify itself, the way fertility does with a mule? Can magic even be passed down through bloodlines and breeding? If it can, how is the potency affected, if at all? You may even have magic abilities conflict with and ultimately weaken one another, as seen in *My Hero Academia*.

SAMPLE FAE/ELF PUNNETT SQUARE

	F	f
E	EF	Ef
e	Fe	ef

Punnett Square of possible Elf/Fae mix. You get to decide what magic goes on which gene.

If magic comes from deities (see next section), how is it passed to their offspring? Are offspring considered lesser or minor gods, and does that affect the magic? What of demigods or half-gods, or the mixing of a god and a mortal (or god and other creatures, such as the aforementioned fae and elves)?

For example:

DEITY MAGIC

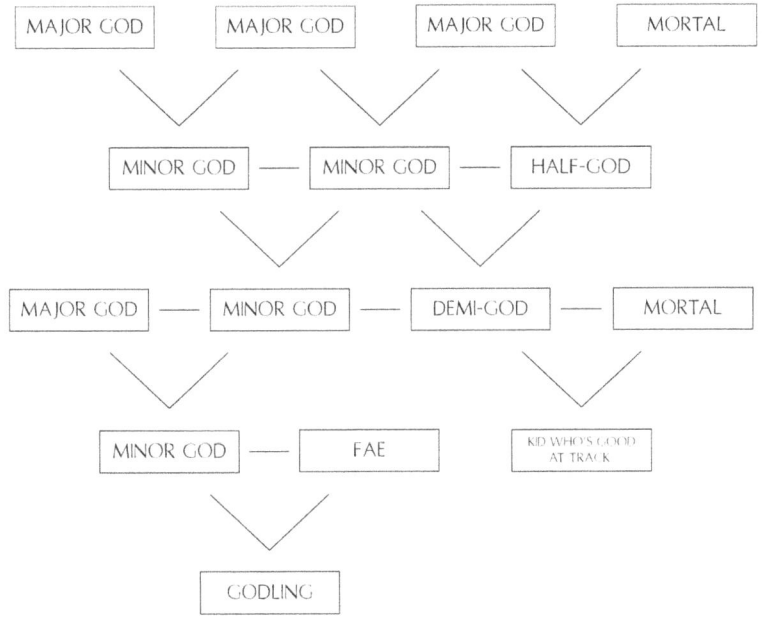

There are blank lineage charts at the end of this chapter for your personal use.

Divine Magic

Divine magic is magic that comes from higher, supernatural beings, usually referred to, simply, as "gods." Novels such as *The Hundred Thousand Kingdoms* by N.K. Jemisin and *The Invisible Life of Addie LaRue* by V.E. Schwab sport magic sourced from gods. Many paranormal stories likewise feature heavily conflicted magic via making a "deal with the devil." Often in books like these, gods are the *only* source of magic, but that limitation is not a requirement for divine magic to work.

When working with gods, we have to ask ourselves a few questions:

- What domain does this god have? (Especially critical for polytheistic stories.)

- What powers or abilities does the god possess?

- Are gods immortal?

- What form, if any, does this god take?

- Where does this god fit in a class system, among mortals and among her own ilk?

- What impact does the existence of this god have on the worldbuilding and the story?

- Does the god have to be present for the magic to happen, or are they bequeathing it to the magic user?

In *The Wings Upon Her Back* by Samantha Mills, gods are the source of magic, the source of religion, and even the source of advanced technology. Magicked tech is gifted by the god central to the story, the Mecha God, to worthy followers.

JUST A SPRINKLE

Note that you absolutely can have gods in your story without the magic system revolving around them. Gods can exist and have their own flavor of magic without their magic directly affecting the plot. Or, they can simply be deity used in religion and oaths who are never actually characters in a story. If you want to use gods, the choice is entirely yours.

Magic Talismans

Magic may also come in the form of a physical object, or a *magical talisman*. Magical talismans are tangible things imbued with magic. These are really handy when it comes to limitations, because they have a quantifiable source of magic, are often transferrable, and have the potential to be lost or stolen. Talismans can contain a single spell or specific type of power, or they can be the power source for a range of abilities. For example, the earrings in *Miraculous Ladybug*, or the pen in *Sailor Moon*, contain a spectrum of magic for their magic users to tap into—in both cases, they are transformative magic that then provides an arsenal of "spells" for our superheroes to access in battle. On the other hand, the cap from *Mighty Max* and the sword from T. Kingfisher's *Swordheart* have a very specific ability (the first being the ability to teleport via portals, and the second being the ability to store and transfer your own personal bodyguard).

The talismans mentioned above are what I call *abso-*

lute talismans, meaning the magic, in its entirety, is tied into the imbued object. One hundred percent. If Ladybug loses her earrings, she has zero magic. All her powers are contained in the earrings. However, you can also have a *partial talisman*, where the magic is only partially tied to the object in question. This is something that, while containing magical properties, only a magic user can wield (it doesn't inherently have magic). An example of a partial talisman is Gandalf's staff in The Lord of the Rings series. Gandalf can cast magic with or without his staff; his access to magic is not dependent on his having his talisman in hand. It's just a helpful tool. (In this case, the staff is more of a conduit than a necessity.)

If we want to get nitpicky with talismans, we can also separate them into *dependent* and *independent* categories. Dependent talismans require a magic user to make them work; they are not magical in and of themselves. For example, Dudley from the Harry Potter series can't grab Harry's wand and suddenly be able to cast spells—he isn't a wizard. On the other hand, independent talismans contain the entirety of magic within them, and anyone can use it. The seven-league boots from European folklore, introduced to me personally via Dianna Wynne Jones's *Howl's Moving Castle*[16], allows their wearer to travel seven leagues in a single step. Anyone off the street can put these boots on and use this magic, regardless of their magical history (or lack thereof).

---

16 Sheesh, Charlie. You sure talk about this book a lot. (Yes I do. And it's a wonderful book.)

Witches and Wizardry

The terms "witches" and "wizards" are very commonly used for magic users throughout all forms of media. However, when I refer to *witches and wizardry* as a template of magic, I am referring to the very classical broad-enchantment, read-a-spellbook, wave-a-wand type of magic. In this type of magic, spellbooks (and sometimes magical talismans) are very necessary, if not entirely necessary, to cast magic.

In *The Wizard of Earthsea* by Ursula K. Le Guin, wizards use *The Book of Names* to learn and access their magic. Jonathan Stroud's Bartimaeus trilogy utilizes spellbooks (grimoires) to share the knowledge of summoning and controlling demons[17]. One could even argue that Margaret Rogerson's *Sorcery of Thorns* can fall under this category, though her grimoires truly do take on a life of their own.

I dare say that this classic template of magic even extends to the popular fictional use of witchcraft through herbology, where different plants can be used to create different spells or magical effects. This magic usually, on page or off, comes with a recipe "spellbook" of sorts. One example of herbology-style witchcraft is *Salt and Broom* by Sharon Lynn Fisher, though her competent protagonist has memorized her herbology notes by the time the story starts.

---

17 The only way to use magic at all in this world is via demons, so one could argue that, in this instance, demons are living talismans (and exclusive magic).

Component Magic

Sometimes magic needs components for a spell to work—this is brushing up against the herbology magic mentioned in the *Witches and Wizardry* section. However, using a component is different than using a talisman— wherein the talisman itself is magical, the component is merely fodder. In the case of physical components, think of magic as a creature that needs to be fed. If you don't have the exact foods the creature wants to eat, it's not going to do as you ask.

For example, in *Dealing with Dragons* by Patricia C. Wrede, Cimorene and Alianora must acquire specific components for a variation on a dragon spell. These components include, specifically, wolfsbane, unicorn water, and white eagle feathers.

Another familiar type of magic that falls under the style of the "component" category is that of linguistics. Magic requiring spoken or written word in one form or another is common because it's understandable. Linguistic components reach outside mere spellbooks, however; they can require a vast understanding of language, such as in *Babel* by R.F. Kuang.

In *Babel*, magic is found in the translation of words— the spaces between true meaning when translating one language into another—and using words that share similar space. This magic *only* works if the magic user is fluent in both languages they are using in translation.

On the other hand, we have spells that must be written for the magic to work. Written linguistic magic can be long-form or short, whichever works for the story (having long-form writing is a great way to add a limitation to a magic system, since it costs time). Runic magic falls under this category as well.

A great example of written linguistic magic is The Founders Trilogy by Robert Jackson Bennett. This series utilizes written runic magic known as sigils, which are used to coerce inanimate objects to behave contrary to their nature (like getting carriage wheels to spin on their own). But Bennett takes his magic system beyond scrawling a single rune on an object to make magic happen—the instructions must be very clear for the object to understand what it's meant to do. Clarity requires a lot of words/sigils, to the point where some objects simply aren't large enough to contain the entirety of a magic user's desired instructions. And so magic users created lexicons, which are essentially a fantasy version of a data center: they're full of explanations written out in sigils. So now, when a magic user wants to enchant an object, they can write simplified sigils essentially telling the object to look up its instructions in the server.

Sympathetic Magic

An established magic belief in the real-world, sympathetic magic (also called "imitative" magic) is the idea that magic can be formed through representation or symbolism—something figuratively standing in for a person or thing on which, or for which, you want the magic to be performed. One of the most well-known examples of this is the Haitian folk tradition of Voodoo dolls, where acts performed on the dolls are believed to occur to the person the doll represents. Something similar can be seen in the climax of movie adaptation of Neil Gaiman's *Stardust,* when a doll representation of the character Septimus is used to control the man, even after his death. One could even argue that Oscar Wilde's *The Picture of Dorian Gray* is sympathetic magic, though magic is never truly pinned down in that novel (and it falls under the category of magical realism, as discussed in the next section).

Sympathetic magic also applies to the previously mentioned component magic system, where different components represent, or stand in for, different traits or abilities. For instance, the herb rosemary is believed to represent purity in many traditions, so it would be used to cast spells that require a representation of purity.

In a nutshell, the equation for sympathetic magic is "like = like," which is widely used in modern-day witchcraft.

Uncanny Magic

Remember that TV show *Stan Lee's Superhumans*? Yes? This is where we're headed with this style of magic system. No? You'll catch up real quick.

Uncanny magic is magic that's believable, or magic that's close enough to the realm of normalcy that it's easy for us to extend our believability. Things *slightly* super-human.

Popular uncanny magic includes heightened senses (*Daredevil*), physical abilities (super strength, speed … I mean, who here doesn't think Usain Bolt is just a little magical), mental (*Long Island Medium*), or spiritual (*Ghost Talkers* by Mary Robinette Kowal) abilities. Stories like *The Sixth Sense* and Maggie Stiefvater's *The Scorpio Races* all fall under uncanny magic. This magic is great for authors and readers who have a hard time accepting something is magic "just because," and often lends to a wider readership because the magic system has a shallow learning curve.

- Magical Realism

   When we step outside uncanny magic just enough that we can no longer believe this is the real-world, we step into magical realism.
   Magical realism is a light-dusting-of-fantasy subgenre that usually takes place in the world as we know it, but there's one element of magic within its confines. Examples of this include "A Very Old Man with Enormous Wings" by Gabriel García Márquez, where a man with wings, thought to be an angel, visits a normal fishing village; the Outlander series by Diana Gabaldon, where a woman finds a passageway into the past; and *Shoeless Joe* by W. P. Kinsella (made into the popular movie *Field of Dreams*), where a man builds a baseball diamond to receive angelic visitors.

Magic That Isn't

I've said it once, and I'll say it again—a fantasy novel doesn't require magic. It can be otherworld or have otherly characters. Something that makes it fantastically different from the world as we know it. Which also means your "magic system" doesn't have to have supernatural roots.

Take Mark Twain's *Connecticut Yankee in King Author's Court*. This is a fantasy novel, as it involves time travel to the 400s, but the magic the protagonist, Hank, uses in the story is purely scientific (such as using a calendar to predict the occurrence of a solar eclipse, and pretending *he* is the one blocking out the sun.) Yet for people living in the fifth century, modern-day science would seem completely supernatural. That, and the fact that we don't know for certain if Hank actually traveled to the past, or if it was all an intense dream, lends to the idea that this magic may be make-believe.

Another example of magic-that-isn't is (and this is a spoiler for the novel, so if you haven't read *Warrior of the Wild* by Tricia Levenseller and plan to, just skip to the next section) *Warrior of the Wild* by Tricia Levenseller. The tyrannical "god" in this story uses the power of magnets, not the supernatural, to cow others to his will. The "magic system" is treated wholly as real magic until the truth is revealed near the end of the novel.

Also, every episode of *Scooby-Doo* ever made[18].

---

18 Except possibly Scooby Doo on Zombie Island, as one of my beta readers pointed out to me.

Lineage Charts

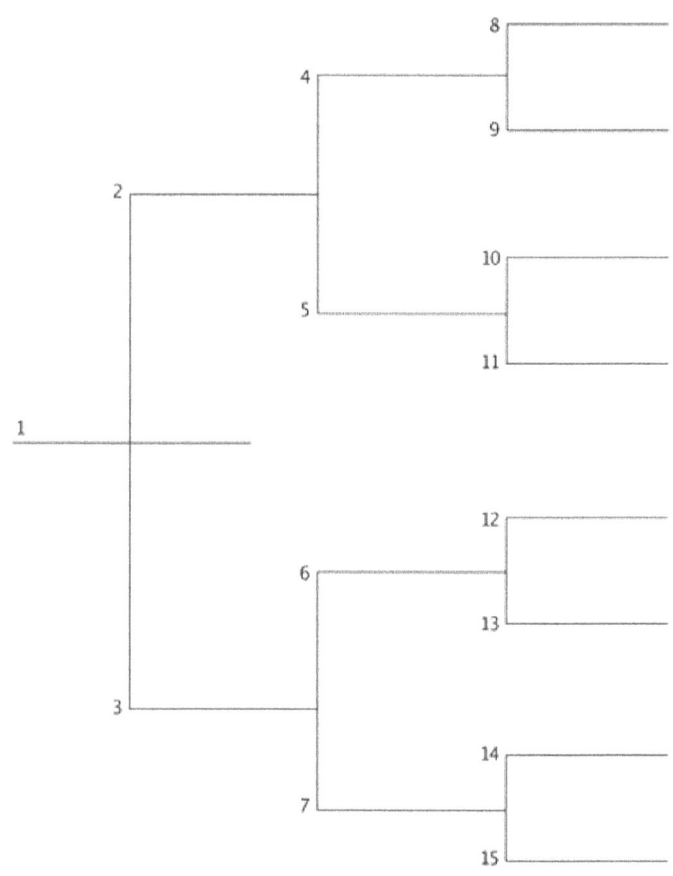

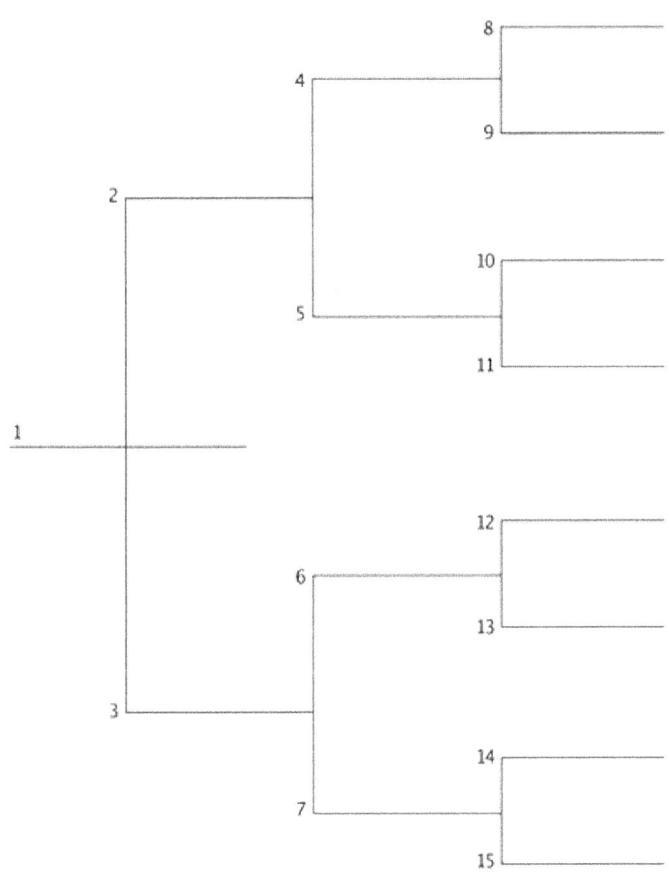

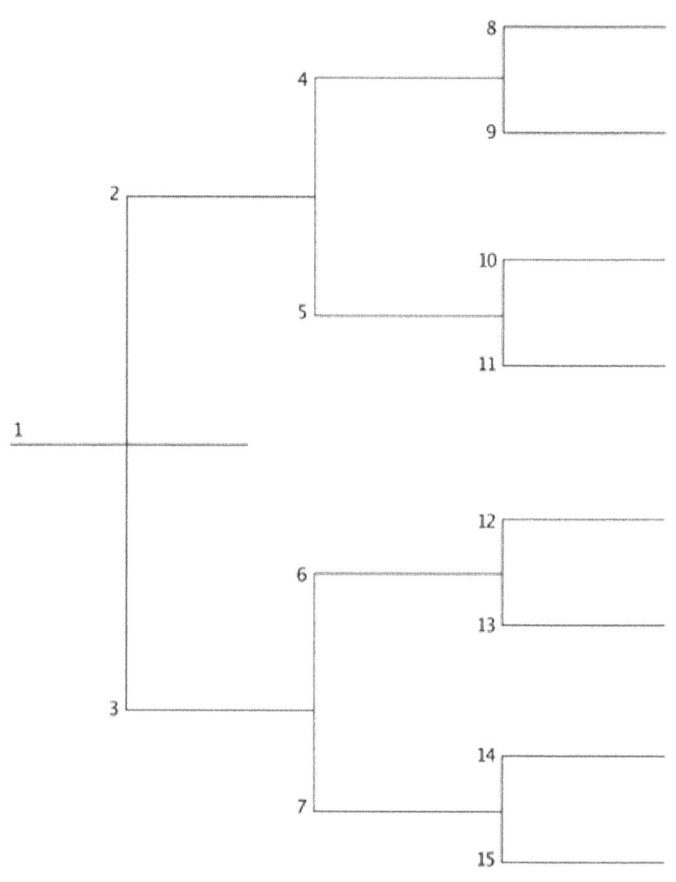

Notes:

_____

_____

_____

_____

_____

_____

_____

_____

_____

_____

_____

_____

_____

_____

_____

_____

_____

_____

_____

_____

7
PIECING IT TOGETHER

"One doesn't need magic if one knows enough stories."

—*Emily Wilde's Encyclopedia of Faeries* by Heather Fawcett

How to Come Up with the Stuff

So, you want to write a cool magic system, but you don't know where to start. What kind of magic is *cool*? What can you do that interests you? If the workshops and worksheets in this book don't get the mental juices flowing, and the appendices at the end of the book aren't lighting any bulbs, try asking yourself the following questions:

- *What* looks *cool?* If it's visually appealing in your head, it might be more exciting to write.

- *What best serves the plot or the characters?* If you know the type of story you want to tell, what kind of magic would best lend to it?

- *What serves the worldbuilding?* If you've already developed your setting, brainstorm what sort of magic complements it. If you haven't built out your world yet, try starting there.

- *What mystery of the universe can you play with?* This might be where the planetary rings came from, why sound ceases to exist the moment you leave the kingdom, or why second-borns end up dying at the age of fifteen. This relates back to worldbuilding—build out some mysteries, then see if you can use magic to solve them.

- *What classic magic can you remake?* If there is a common or old-school magic system you like, see if there's an interesting spin you can put on it.

- *What supernatural spin can you put on something that interests you?* Are you really into rock-climbing, cooking, or jewelry making? Perhaps there's something in one of your interests or hobbies that can be reconfigured with the fantastic in mind.

- *Who did it* wrong? Listen. We've all had a book we've read or a movie we've watched and thought, *well if* I *were writing this story, I'd do X instead.* If you've seen a magic system you felt didn't live up to its potential, and it's not crossing obvious copyright boundaries, remake it to appeal to you.

- *What would be fun to write?* If having characters throw fireballs at each other entices you, then find a way for your characters to throw fireballs.

A lot of us get ideas for a certain ability or power and build out our magic systems from there. However, there is no correct order for creating a magic system—you can start wherever you want. But if you're hitting a wall with magic, try brainstorming in another area, such as limitations or acquisitions, instead.

Giving It a Name

I like to give my magic and my magic users titles and terms pretty early on in my writing process so I can have clear labels throughout my story notes. I cannot tell you how many times I've looked up words like "wizard" in the thesaurus and gone down a winding rabbit hole of linguistics. So how do you decide what to call your … things?

Keep it classic. If you call someone a mage, magician, witch, or wizard in your book, we all automatically know they're a magic-user. There's nothing wrong with using established English terms in your story—no one is going to cry out a lack of originality. Same goes for the magic. You can flat-out say they're using spells, incantations, enchantments … even simply "magic."

Change the spelling. "Magick." Or "magique," or "majick," or what have you. You can take known terms and tweak the spelling to suit your needs.

Thesaurus rabbit hole. Look up a term relevant to magic in general, or the abilities you want to use, and hunt around. Places like Thesaurus.com, OneLook.com, and even AI can help you filter through words until you find something you like.

Choose the obvious. Sometimes we don't have to think real hard about terms because the relevant ones are just so … relevant. If you have magic with threads, your magic-users might be called "sewers." If you have magic with plants, they might be called "sowers" (see what I did there?).

Draw from other languages. Raise your hand if you've looked up the Latin translations for various magic terms in an attempt to be "original." (Yes, I have done this. Many times.) Play around in a translation app and see if there's a term from another tongue that appeals to you. Just make sure you're doing it tastefully—inspiration trumps wholesale. You can also tweak those terms to come up with something original (swap a few letters around, marry together different prefixes and suffixes, and so on).

Just … make it up. It's a fantasy novel, for crying out loud. Just smash some letters together that sound good and go with it! Your *Ju'ilil* can perform their *hatcha* rites so they can use the *verini* and beat the bad guy.

In Conclusion

Writing fantasy is hard.

It's easy, in a way. You get to make stuff up to suit your whims. Random guard in the hallway? His name is Geothanus. For no other reason than because that's the first fake name that came to your head.

But while so much of the genre centers on an author's individual creative well, there's a lot that can go wrong. You can plant an active volcano in the middle of the capital, but you still need a reason why someone would build a city around a dangerous lava-spewing mountain. You can sprinkle dragons throughout the countryside, but you still need to determine how they would fit into the ecosystem as a whole. You can write about mermaids, but still have to figure out how exactly they can withstand the pressure of the deep sea in Act 1 but be able to surface without trouble in Act 3.

I've stated throughout this book that magic is a great creator or amplifier for conflict in story and can enhance setting, plot, and character. But magic also complicates things. It can introduce difficulties into your story that may prove frustrating to iron out. But magic can also create a sense of wonder and the feel of the truly fantastic. How many of us, as kids (or, truthfully, as adults) haven't wished we had superpowers of some kind? Who watched X-Men in the nineties and despite all the horrible ways mutants were treated, wished we were a mutant because *it's just so cool*?

Give magic a chance. Dare to explore the unexplored. Wow your readers and *have fun* with it. Take your time, think it out, and then let it explode on the page. Follow your heart, fellow authors. Because when you love something that much, someone else is bound to love it too.

Reading and writing, in and of themselves, are magical. Now is your chance to make them magnificent.

Abracadabra.

The End[19].

---

19 Except for the appendices and the index. I'm sorry, did I ruin that magical finishing moment with this footnote?

8
APPENDICES

A quick introduction to the appendices of this book. These are meant to help in your magic-making journey. The lists are not exhaustive but meant to be tools to spur creative thinking.

Appendix A. This is a list of potential fuels and costs for magic. Because many fuels and costs can be used interchangeably, especially when one likes to think outside the box, I combined them into one list.

Appendix B. These are magic powers and abilities that I see commonly utilized in fantasy. They're a great place to start if you want a shallow learning curve to your magic system, if you want to take a familiar idea and put your own twist on it, or if you want to take a leap toward originality by avoiding them all together.

Appendix C. These are magic types and terms that are well-known in our world. They're words one can find in the dictionary or easily search on Google. However, many of the definitions offered in this appendix are over-simplified. If something interests you or catches your eye, I recommend researching it further on your own.

Appendix D. This is literally a list of random things to help kickstart brainstorming if you don't know where to start with your magic system. It's also useful for completing the workshop at the end of Chapter 4.

Appendix A: Fuel/Costs

Aging
  Growth stunting, intellect stunting
Alchemic properties; something of equal value
Ammunition
Animal parts
  Whiskers, teeth, fur, bones, eyes, claws, talons,
  feathers, scales
Animals
  Presence, sacrifice
Apathy
Appendages
  Body parts, hair
Appetite
Beans
Beauty
Blood
Body parts
Breath
Charisma
Color(s)
Comfort
Confusion
Creativity
  Ability to be creative, creations (paintings,
  sculptures, stories)
Curse
Darkness
Death
Debt
Determination

Dexterity
Dignity
Discomfort
Dreams
    Aspirations, night visions
Drink
    Alcohol, tonics, cocktails, brews, milks,
    other liquids
Drugs
    illegal/legal, herbs, medicines
Ecstasy
Education
Emotion
Emotion, gained
Emotion, loss of
Empathy
Energy
Fainting
Fatigue/energy
Fever
Food
Free will
Gems
    Rare stones, pearls, shells, cut, uncut
Glass
Grace
Health
    Physical, emotional, mental
Herbs
Hygiene
Illness
Inhibition, loss of
Injury/condition

Intelligence
    Books read, questions asked, something
    new learned
Kinetic power
Knowledge
Labor/work
Language
Life
Light
Love
    Loved ones or things
Mana
Memory
Mental capacity
Metal
Mobility
Money
Mutation
Mutilation
Natural resources
    Oil, gas, fossil fuels, coal, wood
Neurological penalties
Nonprecious metals
Oils
Pain
Plants
    Fruit, bark, roots, sap, seed, blooms, pollen,
    fungi, leaves, petals, trees, flowers, berries,
    thorns, poison, smoked, tea, herbs
Pleasure
Precious metals
Promises/oaths
Sacrifice

    Bugs, animals, people, plants
Scrolls
Secrets
Senses
    Sight, hearing, scent, taste, touch
Shadows
Sleep
Smoke
Social standing
Something valued
Speech
Spirit
Strength
Sun
Talismans
Technology
Temperature changes
Time
Twin suffering (double-edged sword, you
experience the same thing you deal out)
Vomiting
Water
Waves
    Radio, x-ray, gamma, light, ocean,
    hand gestures
Weather
    Rain, snow, sunshine, clouds, wind, storms, etc.
Wit
Working memory
Years
Youth
    Youth of others, youth of self

Appendix B: Common Magical Abilities

Animal familiars
Black magic
Colors
Divination
Elements
Enhanced physical abilities (senses, intelligence)
Enhanced physical traits (speed, strength, dexterity)
Glamor
Healing
Herbalism
Kinesis
Legendary creatures
Mindreading
Nature manipulation
Necromancy
Pantheon
Potion-making
Psychic abilities
Runic magic
Shapeshifting
Singing
Spellbook incantation
Teleportation
Time travel
Vampirism
Wand/Staff
Werewolfism
White magic
Witchcraft

Appendix C: Established Magic

Ablution	Cleansing, often ritualistic or religious, with water or other liquids.
Alchemy	Chemistry of transmuting one thing into another, usually a common substance with a rare one, i.e. lead into gold.
Animism	The idea that living things or things of nature possess souls.
Aphrodisiac	Potion, food, drug, or likewise that creates physical arousal.
Astral projection	Projection of the inner self; the idea that the soul or the consciousness can exist outside of, or separate from, the physical body.
Astrology	Belief that celestial bodies, and their placement in the universe, affects humankind on a personal level.
Augury	Divination, future-seeing.
Black magic	Magical abilities used for selfish or evil purposes; opposite of White magic.
Ceremonial	Ritual or long-form casting of magic.
Chaos	Belief, or altering of beliefs, and manipulation of rituals, symbols, and other techniques to achieve a desired outcome.

Chronomancy	Used both as foresight as to what day or time is best for a chosen activity, and as the magical manipulation of time.
Clairvoyance	Insight into the things or people around you; extra-sensory perception.
Conjuration	Evoking or calling upon magical creatures, ghosts, and spiritual beings; also known as evocation.
Contagious	Another term for sympathetic magic, or like = like.
Demonology	Study of, or belief in, demons.
Divination	Reading or foretelling future events or uncovering secret knowledge through magical means (There are many types of divination, each with their own name which are not included in this list).
Dowsing	Act of divining scientific implements, often two rods.
Dream reading	Using images in dreams to determine the health, emotional issues, and future prospects of the dreamer or the dreamed-of.
Dreamwalking	Ability to enter and manipulate the dreams of others.
Elementalism	Magic that stems through the four elements—fire, earth, water, and air. A fifth element, spirit, is often included.

Esotericism	Study or practice of hidden or secret knowledge that holds a mystical, spiritual, or religious significance.
Evocation	Evoking or calling upon magical creatures, ghosts, and spiritual beings; also known as conjuration.
Exorcism	Expulsion of spirits.
Extrasensory perception (ESP)	Ability to gain information through the mind, as opposed to the five senses.
Familiar spirit	Supernatural beings who aid or protect magic users in witchcraft.
Foresight	Seeing something before its occurrence.
Fortune-telling	Predicting a person's luck, future, and/or life.
Geomancy	Manipulation of earth with the mind.
Glamour	Use of enchantment to enhance or change appearance, usually toward that of attractiveness.
Graphology	Study of handwriting to determine one's character and personality.
Gray magic	Neutral magic; magic not performed for beneficial or detrimental purposes.
Herbalism	Use of plants and fungi in medicinal practices; in magic, taking those practices to extremes.
Hydromancy	Ability to manipulate water with the mind.

Hypermnesia	Vivid and accurate recollection of past events.
Illusion	Creating of an image or other sensory phenomena to mislead.
Incantation	Spellcasting with an emphasis on spoken word and the manner in which the words are said.
Invocation	Supplication of a supernatural being.
Low	Magic conducted from grimoires and spellbooks.
Mediumship	Act of being a spiritual medium.
Metaphysics	Study and examination of the structure of reality.
Mysticism	Becoming one with deity or entering an altered state of mind with religious or spiritual intent.
Natural magic	Umbrella terms for magics associated with the natural world.
Necromancy	Magic associated with death and decay.
Oneironautics	Ability to travel through or affect one's own dream.
Ouiji	Use of a letterboard to communicate with spirits, usually during a seance.
Palmistry	Determining one's character or future from the lines and shapes in the palm the hand.

Photokinesis	The ability to manipulate or control light with the mind.
Phrenology	The study of bumps of the skull to determine personality or character traits.
Physiognomy	Using outward appearance to determine character and personality traits.
Planar	Ability to pass between separate planes of existence.
Precognition	Clairvoyance in something yet to occur.
Prophecy	Foresight, foreseeing.
Psionics	The ability to affect and manipulate the world through powers of the mind.
Psychometry	Ability to sense an object's history through touch.
Psychonautics	Meditation or drugs that allow a person to enter a mind-altered state.
Pyrokinesis	Ability to control fire with the mind.
Remote viewing	Sensing aspects of a distant or unseen object with the mind.
Ritual	Ceremonial or long-form casting of magic.
Runic	Magic cast via written word, letters, or symbols.
Scrying	Divination, often with a physical object, such as a crystal ball.

Séance	A means of communicating with spirits.
Seership	The ability to use spiritual, moral, and future sight.
Shapeshifting	The ability to transmute from one form or state to another.
Soothsaying	Divination, foretelling of events, prophecy.
Spiritual possession	Using one's own body, or the body of another, to host a supernatural being.
Summoning	Calling upon a supernatural force or being.
Sympathetic	Magic of "like = like," where something stands in for or represents the desired magical outcome or represents the being on which the magic is to be cast upon.
Tarot reading	Divination through a tarot deck of cards; form of cartomancy.
Telekinesis	The ability to move physical objects or apply physical force with the power of the mind.
Telepathy	Communication from mind to mind; mindreading.
Teleportation	Instantaneous travel between two points without crossing the intervening space between.
Thaumaturgy	The ability to perform miracles; wonderworking.

Theophany	The physical manifestation of a deity.
Theurgy	The ability to persuade god.
Thought-ography	Projected thermography, the ability to burn images from one's mind onto something physical.
Transmutation	Shapeshifting, metamorphosis from one state or form to another.
White magic	Magical abilities used for selfless or noble purposes; opposite of Black magic.
Xenoglossy	The ability to read, write, or speak —outside natural means— a foreign language.

Appendix D:
The Appendix of Random Things to
Help Kickstart Your Brainstorming

Adhesive

Adoption

Adrenaline

Alcohol

Alphabet

Altitude

Amphibians

Animal skins

Antlers

Arachnids

Arrows

Art

Ash

Bacteria

Balance

Balloons

Baskets

Baths

Beads

Beans

Birdsong

Birthdays

Board games

Bodies of water

Bombs

Bones

Bongs

Bottles

Braiding

Bread

Bridges

Bubbles

Butter

Cacti

Cakes

Calendars

Calluses

Cameras

Campfires

Candles

Candy

Cardinal directions

Cards

Cast iron

Caves

Celestial bodies

Centripetal force

Ceramics

Chains

Charity

Children

Cigars

Clay

Clocks

Cloth

Clothing

Clouds

Cocktails

Cogs

Communication devices

Compass

Compliments

Computers

Confidence

Construction material

Corners

Cosmetics

Cousins

Criticism

Crowns/tiaras

Cups

Curiosity

Dawn

Debate

Decibels

Dentistry

Depth

Desire

Dice

Discovery

Disease

Distance

Division

Dolls

Doors

Dust

Earthworms

Eggs

Electrons

Embers

Embroidery

Emojis

Enlightenment

Epiphany

Exploration

Eyes

Faith

Fans

Fashion

Feathers

Files

Fingerprints

Fishing

Flowers

Footwear

Forests

Forgiveness

Fossils

Freckles

Fruit

Fungi

Fur

Furniture

Games

Gasoline

Generosity

Ghosts

Gifts

Glue

Grammar

Gratitude

Guilt

Hair

Hand tools

Hatred

Hats

Hearts

Holes

Holidays

Hooves

Horns

Houses

Humility

Hunting

Hyperbole

Ice

Imagination

Ink

Insects

Insurance

Intellect

Intimacy

Jellyfish

Jewelry

Journals

Judgement

Keyboards

Keys

Kisses

Knifework

Knives

Knowledge

Labor

Lace

Ladders

Lamps

Laws

Leaves

Letters

Light sources

Lightbulbs

Literature

Locks

Lures

Magnets

Maps

Marbles

Mazes

Measurement

Medicines

Menstruation

Mental illness

Milk

Mining

Mirrors

Moles

Money

Moon phases

Mosaics

Motion

Motivation

Mud

Mummies

Musical instru-
ments

Musical notation

Nails

Natural disasters

Needles

Numbers

Nuts

Oaths

Oil

Optimism

Orbs/globes

Paintings

Paper

Pastry

Paths

Patterns

Pawprints

Pebbles

Peels

Pens

Perfume

Periodic table

Pessimism

Photos

Piano keys

Picture frames

Piercings

Pies

Pinecones

Plasma

Plays

Poetry

Poison

Porcelain

Portraits

Potpourri

Preservatives

Pressure

Pride

Prisms

Promises

Puzzles

Pyramids

Quilts

Recyclables

Reptiles

Revelation

Rhymes

Ribbons

Rings

Rivers

Rodents

Rope

Salt

Sandpaper

Saplings

Scales

Seeds

Self-esteem

Sewing

Shapes

Ships/boats

Siblings

Skulls

Smoke

Snowflakes

Soap

Software

Spectacles

Speech

Spinners

Spoons

Springs

Stairs

Statues

Steps

Sticks

Stitching

Stones

Sugar

Surgery

Sweat

Sympathy

Tea

Tears

Technology

Teeth

Thorns

Thread

Trash

Travel

Trophies

Truth

Twilight

UV rays

Video

Viruses

Vitamins

Wainscotting

Walls

Weapons

Webs

Weddings

Weight

Wheels

Windows

Wings

Wires

Wisdom

Wonder

Wood

Woodgrain

Woodworking

Wool

Wrinkles

References

Bennett, Robert Jackson. Foundryside (The Founders Trilogy Book 1). Dey Ray. 2018.

Farland, David. The Runelords Series. Tor Fantasy. 1999.

Fawcett, Heather. Emily Wilde's Encyclopaedia of Faeries (p. 195). Random House Worlds. Kindle Edition.

Gillig, Rachel. One Dark Window (The Shepherd King Series Book 1). Orbit. Print Edition.

Gornichec, Genevieve. The Witch's Heart (p. 185). Penguin Publishing Group. Kindle Edition.

Harmon, Amy. The Bird and the Sword (The Bird and the Sword Chronicles Book 1). Createspace. 2016.

Jemisin, N.K.. The Hundred Thousand Kingdoms (The Inheritance Trilogy Book 1) (p. 49). Orbit. Kindle Edition.

Jones, Dianna Wynne. Howl's Moving Castle (Howl's Moving Castle Book 1). Greenwillow Books of New York. 1986.

Kuang, R.F. Babel, Or, The Necessity of Violence: An Arcane History of the Oxford Translators' Revolution. Harper Voyager. 2022.

Levenseller, Tricia. Warrior of the Wild. Feiwel & Friends. 2019.

McClellan, Brian. In The Shadow of Lightning (Glass Immortals Book 1). Tor Book. 2022.

McFarland, Caitlyn. Soul of Smoke: A Dragon Shifter Romance (Dragonsworn Book 1) . Carina Press. Kindle Edition.

Meyer, Stephenie. Twilight (The Twilight Saga Book 1). Little, Brown and Company. 2005.

Prince, S.G.. To Poison a King (Heirs of Isla) (p. 116). Summerhold Publishing. Kindle Edition.

Rowling, J.K. The Harry Potter Series. Bloomsbury. 1997.

Smith, Luanne G.. The Witch's Lens: A Novel (The Order of the Seven Stars Book 1) (p. 128). 47North. Kindle Edition.

Sanderson, Brandon. "What Are Sanderson's Laws of Magic?" Brandonsanderson.com. Dragonsteel Publishing. 2018. https://faq.brandonsanderson.com/knowledge-base/what-are-sandersons-laws-of-magic/.

Sanderson, Brandon. The Mistborn Series. Tor Books. 2006.

Sanderson, Brandon. The Alloy of Law (The Wax & Wayne Series, Book 1). Tor Books. 2011.

Weeks, Brent. The Lightbringer Series. Orbit. 2010.

Wees, Alyssa. Nocturne: A Novel (p. 144). Random House Worlds. Kindle Edition.

Wheeler, Jeff. The Muirwood Series. 47North. 2011.

INDEX

ACKNOWLEDGEMENTS

I had the idea for this book kicking around in my head for a little while. Like a good story idea, it stuck, and eventually I found myself heading to my computer to write it. However, though this book is notably shorter than my usual novels, it took a real TEAM to piece it together. You can't just make stuff up in nonfiction. You have to know things. So, first, I want to thank all the people who helped me with my research and subsequently made my life much easier: Jordan Holmberg, Kristy Stewart, Andrew Stevens, Cathy Webb, Kayley Klindt, Erin Barrow, Amy Lauderback, Caitlyn McFarland, Brent Weeks, Jeff Wheeler, Robert Bennett, Brian McClellan, and Andrew Tolman.

I also want to thank my beta readers for combing through this and helping with those final touches! Much appreciation to Amy Lauderback, Dustin McClain, Kanisha Chandler, Leah O'Neill, Rhonda Lind, Megan Richards, Andrew Stevens, Deborah Deichter, and Daphne Tatum.

So much gratitude goes to Tanya Crosby-Straley and the team at Oliver Heber Books. Not only are they my OB-GYN for this book, but they went outside their comfort zone to publish nonfiction for me. Y'all are great.

And, in reference to the section on divine magic in Chapter 6, many thanks to God for giving me literally the coolest job ever. Though if anyone ever needs me to be a judge on a cake show, I will happily take the position.

ABOUT THE AUTHOR

Charlie N. Holmberg is a *Wall Street Journal* and Amazon Charts bestselling author of fantasy and romance fiction, including the Paper Magician series, the Spellbreaker series, and the Whimbrel House series, and writes contemporary romance under C. N. Holmberg. She is published in over twenty languages and is both a Goodreads Choice Award and RITA™ finalist. Born in Salt Lake City, Charlie was raised a Trekkie alongside three sisters who also have boy names. She is a BYU alumna, plays the ukulele, and owns too many pairs of glasses. She currently lives with her family in Utah.

Visit her at www.charlienholmberg.com.

Extra Notes:

_____

_____

_____

_____

_____

_____

_____

_____

_____

_____

_____

_____

_____

_____

_____

_____

_____

_____

_____

_____

_____

_____

Milton Keynes UK
Ingram Content Group UK Ltd.
UKHW030952181124
451360UK00006B/688